MONEY, RICHES &

WEALTH

A biblical perspective on money matters

VOLUME 1

Ricardo Taylor

6/20/2013

Money, Riches & Wealth

Dedication

This book is dedicated to my wife Yolanda, God's

special

gift and to my three children, Delandro, Rickeda

and Daniel, may you continue to

shine like lights in the earth.

TABLE OF CONTENTS

Money, Riches & Wealth

Money, Riches & Wealth

Money, Riches & Wealth

Introduction

A Question of Perspective – Shattering False Mindsets

Let us begin to shatter some false mindsets. Let us get a handle on our world view.

One of the biggest strongholds which remain to be conquered is the management of money and wealth. This remains a tricky area to handle, but it is one in which we can have victory. Since demonic strongholds are mindsets which keep us ignorant to the purposes of God, we need to discover and understand the truth about money and wealth from God's perspective. We need to pray for God to open our understanding so that false mindsets can be exposed and dealt with.

To do this, we can go to the straightforward teaching of Jesus found in Matthew 6:24. There Jesus says that we CANNOT serve God and mammon. Mammon is one of the foundations of the worldly economy and Jesus would have very carefully chosen the Aramaic term "mammon" to illustrate a profound truth. What is mammon? The word mammon is often interpreted as money, but this is inaccurate. The original Aramaic term means confidence in wealth or material wealth or power. Mammon therefore is a spirit of greed and avarice, and money, power or wealth is the ultimate goal.

One of the devil's tricks is to get us to put our confidence in money, riches and material possessions and to serve them by spending our lives reaching for and achieving them. For true citizens of God's kingdom, there is only one master – Yashua or Jesus Christ — and we must be definitely sure that our confidence is only, and always in Him. We must be confident in God's provision, love and care for us. In this passage, Jesus is warning us that if we choose to serve mammon we will end up in bondage as it is impossible to have two masters. Money, riches and wealth are good servants, but they are awful masters. We must be determined, therefore, to learn, with God's help, how to master money and material goods and to properly use them.

> "But remember the LORD your God, for it is he who gives you the ability to produce wealth, and so confirms his covenant, which he swore to your ancestors, as it is today." (Deuteronomy 8:18 NIV)

From the above verse which God spoke to the children of Israel, we know that God is a God of covenant. We also know that this covenant extends to us as children of Abraham. God's covenant to Israel included the ability to produce wealth. Has God changed? The Bible tells us that there is no shadow or turning with God. He is the same today, yesterday and forever. God wanted His people to prosper. Does he still want his people to prosper under the new covenant? Absolutely! Because we are his! Every good father wants what is best for his children and God is the best Father. To properly understand why God wants us to prosper, it is best to first look at the opposite of prosperity. What's the opposite of prosperity? You guessed it — poverty. God is not only good, but He is also a God of abundance. The cattle on a thousand hills belong to him. Poverty does not reflect God's abundant nature. The Oxford English Dictionary defines poverty as follows: "Poverty is the deprivation of food, shelter, money and clothing that occurs when people cannot satisfy their basic needs. Poverty can be understood simply as a lack of money, or more broadly in terms of barriers to everyday life. Absolute poverty or destitution refers to the state of severe deprivation of basic human needs, which commonly includes food, water, sanitation, clothing, shelter, health care, education and information". Poverty does not reflect God's abundant nature. When parents have to put their children to bed without anything to eat as happens in many poor nations, this does not reflect God's abundant nature. When people are forced to steal to find relief from the hardships of life, it brings degradation and slavery. All the wealth generated in the illegal narcotics industry, the liquor and cigarette industries is an affront to God and has resulted in the destruction of many lives and systemic poverty. What is systemic poverty? Ed Silvoso, in his book *Transformation*, defines it as "an all-encompassing socioeconomic structure that keeps people deprived. It exists because of an institutionalized attitude that legitimizes its twin evil premises that some people deserve more opportunity than others, and that there is not much that can or should be done about this prevailing social injustice-similar to how slavery was justified in the past. Because this evil is systemic, it will not be eradicated by simply taking care of individuals at the micro level or providing massive aid at the macro level. It must be uprooted."[1]

The Greek philosopher Aristotle said, "Poverty is the parent of revolution and crime."

Mahatma Gandhi said "Poverty is the worst form of violence."

When the people of God prosper, they should be a blessing to their neighbors, city, nation and the world.

> "When the righteous prosper, the city rejoices;
> Through the blessing of the upright a city is exalted"

---

[1] Ed Silvoso, Transformation (Regal Books 2007) P 116.

(Proverbs 11:10,11 NIV)

Now is the time for the people of God to wake up to the fact that it is not God's will for the world to prosper financially while millions are hungry lost and hurting. God's will is that we, the people of God, prosper and make a difference in the world. God's covenant promise to Abraham in Genesis 12:1-2 was for Abraham to become a great nation and to be a blessing. This is a simple fact of the covenant although prosperity itself is not necessarily always a sign of the blessing of God.

There are many traps to be avoided in relation to money, wealth and riches but we must overcome the spirit of fear, so that we can possess the land of our inheritance. The real purpose of prosperity in the kingdom of God is to have what we need and still be able to give, for God is a giver.

"For God so loved the world that he gave his one and only Son, that whoever believes in him shall not perish but have eternal life."
(John 3:16 NIV)

When we define godly prosperity, we have to start with God's most basic and best gift — His only "Begotten Son". God gave us His best because God is a God of love and because God is a giver. We as children of God must be like our father. We must love people and use money and wealth to expand God's kingdom here on earth. Each of us who know God has a field or assignment to which God has called us. In that field there are many resources which we have to harvest but we have to look to God who is the Lord of the harvest and his ability to supernaturally supply. The most precious resource, however, is not money, silver or gold! The most precious resource is people.

> "What good will it be for someone to gain the whole world, yet forfeit their soul? Or what can anyone give in exchange for their soul?"
> (Matthew 16:26 NIV)

God values the soul of man—even just one man—above all the riches of the world. Therefore, the role of godly prosperity and abundance is so that we can learn how to be good stewards of God's resources and use them for the benefit of His purposes on the earth. We can do this by, first, giving ourselves to Him, and then by giving and sowing into those areas in which the Holy Spirit directs us so that they can increase and expand His kingdom on earth.

This is a new time and a new season! God is giving us strategies for the harvest fields and for greater kingdom impact. The first place God has to start is our minds, to shatter our false mindsets inherited from our spiritual parents that to be poor is spiritual, or that our personal worth is derived from how much money we possess. Listen, our worth is not linked to how much money we have, but to our stewardship and this includes the stewardship of our lives.

God wants to bring us to a place where we are not trying to get, but to give, to a place where we are not a curse but a blessing, to a place where we are not building our own kingdoms but His. God wants for us to put our entire trust in Him and in his ability to supply our needs as El Shaddai, the God who is more than enough. This trust and faith of the heart makes God real to us. If we put our trust in anything else but God we create an idol. When we put our faith and trust in God then our hearts will be protected from the idolatry of mammon which is bound up with trust and false perception of reality. It's a question of worldviews.

Worldviews

Each of us has a pair of lenses through which we see reality, through which we see the world. Our worldview has significant implications for society, and every culture has its own set of "blinders" that prohibit people from seeing all of reality.

What's a world view?

A worldview is a set of assumptions held consciously or unconsciously in faith about the basic makeup of the world and how the world works.[2] In his remarkable book, *Discipling Nations: the power of truth to transform culture*, Darrow L Miller says that everyone has a worldview and it affects what we see, not what there is to be seen. Miller continues, "Worldviews do not stay in the

---

[2] Darrow Miller, Discipling Nations (YWAM Publishing 1998) P 38.

dusty pages of the obscure homes of a professor's library. They are diffused across oceans, through societies, and over the centuries, shaping individuals, cultures, nations and the flow of history. Worldviews spread horizontally. Geographically, they begin with an individual and spread to His disciples, who take the message to the community, to the nation, and ultimately to the world".[3] Since this book is about money, riches and wealth, and since I am a born again believer in Jesus Christ and therefore a member of His church, I want to deal with what has become a skewed, non-biblical world view in the church called dualism.

This worldview separates between the unseen spiritual reality and the earthly related matters pertaining to natural things. Darrow Miller, I believe, explains it best: "Unwittingly, Christians had fallen into the ancient Greek dichotomy dividing the universe into the spiritual realm, which is considered sacred, and the physical, viewed as profane. Faith, theology, ethics, missions, the devotional life, and evangelism were placed in the spiritual realm and

---

[3] Darrow Miller, Discipling Nations (YWAM Publishing 1998) P 39-41

considered of first importance. Reason, science, business, politics, art, music and meeting people's physical needs occupied the lower physical realm. In expressing their desire to serve in missions or the pastorate, Christians often betray their dichotomized thinking when they declare that they want to go into "full-time Christian service", implying that all other Christians engaged in "secular" pursuits, are part-time Christians. Thus, many Christians today suffer from "split personalities". Their lives are divided into compartments: "the religious", which is what they do when attending church or a Bible study; and "the secular", their jobs, recreation and education. Millions of believers operate from this worldview."[4]

Miller calls this Evangelical Gnosticism. It has caused millions of Christians to believe that money and material wealth has nothing to do with the Christian life. But this is not true and contrary to the teaching of the Bible. The Bible makes it clear that the way we use money and other material resources is a litmus test of our spiritual

---

[4] Darrow Miller, Discipling Nations (YWAM Publishing 1998) P 46.

stewardship before God. This will become clearer as we progress through the book.

So Let us start to look at some important money matters because money does matter.

Chapter 1

Money Matters

This book is about money because it is important that people understand money, its purpose, its value and its use. If you can understand money and how it works then it is more likely that you will be able to "make" some more. They are many myths associated with money and because of this many people have been held captive by the lure and desire to accumulate money without coming to a proper understanding of how money is to be used in the development of society.

The development of society involves not only the development of people, but the development and use of its resources. One of the key resources is money, simply because the use of money affects so many other areas. The doctor, the lawyer, the policeman, the pastor, all have to learn how to handle money.

This book deals with money management. You will learn what money really is, where the concept of money came from and how money derives its value.

As a management accountant for over thirty years, I have been involved in money and resource management, but it was as a pastor that I realized the crying need to understand money, its power and how to teach it to God's people. I saw people in bondage to the power and lure of money. I saw the anomaly of the church in dire need for money to carry out its God-given mandate, yet not being able to offer any kind of relevant teaching concerning money for lack of knowledge thereof. For many, money was mammon, worldly and evil, a trap leading directly into the hands of the devil. I saw within the church the sacred/secular division and its detrimental impact to one's view of money.

As I started to learn about the kingdom of God, I discovered that Jesus talked a lot about money and money-related matters in his teachings and parables. Jesus clearly understood that the kingdom of God was about reclaiming all of life for He knew that God made all things for us to enjoy. I became determined to unravel the mystery of money.

The Bible teaches in Hosea 4:6 that God's people are destroyed for lack of knowledge. Lack of knowledge has kept a lot of God's people in bondage for a long time. As God's people are kept in bondage, Satan, the god of this world, maintains control over the world's resources, resources that are needed for the advancement of the Kingdom of God. This book is about bringing change. It starts with a change in mindset. The religious mindset and myths about money must be broken. Money itself may be neutral but it will either be used for good or for evil. It is its use that will determine whether it then can be called good or evil. Here is the greatest opportunity to make a difference.

Jesus puts it this way. "It's more blessed to give than to receive" (Acts20:35). To give whatever you've got. To give of the wealth with which we are born since true wealth is more than money and worldly riches.

Money Matters

There can be no denial of the fact that money is important in the modern society in which we live. Money matters and it has never been more relevant than in our current global economic crisis. The global economic recession has had its impact in 2009, 2010, 2011 and through much of 2012. As we come to the end of 2012, most people continue to take a long hard look at their household expenses as they prepare for what is likely to be still a pretty turbulent year ahead. Some people on the other hand say that they do not care about money, that money is not everything. It's true, money is not everything and you may not care about money but your mortgage company does, the supermarket you shop at does, the clothing store, your beautician or barber all care about your money. To understand why nothing can take the place of money in any area in which money is used one has to understand money and what it is.

What is money?

Many people hold widely divergent views about money. Some view money as the root of all evil and believe that poverty brings one closer to God. Many believe strongly in a "health and wealth" theology which says that Christians are almost automatically destined to become financially successful if not fabulously rich. Most people who hold to these diametrically opposed views think that they both come directly from the Bible. Is money good or evil? To lay a good foundation for managing one's finances it is absolutely imperative to understand what money really is.

Before there was money

Before there was money there was the barter system — the direct exchange of goods and services. One of the primary purposes of money is as a medium of exchange. The concept of money has existed for thousands of years and has taken many forms. Items such as salt, Ivory (elephant's teeth), wampum (beads made from shell), tobacco and even stone have been used as a form of money.

The expression "worth your salt" came from the days of the Roman Empire when its soldiers were paid in salt and they employed the bartering system as means of payment and settling the debt. When a payment was made and the debt paid, there was no remaining obligation between the parties involved in the transaction.

Then money came along. Suppose the world had only two people, a pig farmer and a sugar cane farmer for example. Money would not really be needed! They could simply trade at an agreed exchange rate of sugar per pig! The rate would be determined by the relative supply of each commodity. Now add a vegetable farmer, an elephant-Ivory trader, a tobacco manufacturer, a cow farmer, a sheep farmer, a carpenter and a clothes maker and, suddenly, there are simply too many exchange rates to keep track of.

Money smoothed the mechanism of exchange and solved the problem of trying to determine how much a half a pig was worth in relation to a sack of sugar or Elephant's teeth. Money is not just used as a medium of exchange; it also serves as a unit of account. By selling the pigs and the sugar for money all prices can now be expressed in the common dollars and cents.

Store of value

Besides being a medium of exchange and a unit of account, money is also a store of value. Any commodity that can be held and exchanged later for goods and services is called a store of value.

For example, if the pig farmer sells all of his surplus pigs, but does not need to buy sheep right away, he can simply "store" the proceeds from his sales as money by depositing the money in the bank. This money becomes his store of value. The more stable the value of a commodity, the better it can act as a store of value and the more useful it is as money. No store of value is completely safe, however, and the value of a physical object such as a house, a car or a work of art, will fluctuate over time. Many people prefer to store their money in land or "real estate", which is extremely stable and tends to increase in value over time, unlike a car which decreases in value over time.

Characteristics of Good Money

Here are characteristics of good money.

1.   The supply must be constant and not scarce.

2.   Good money would be difficult to counterfeit.

3.   Good money is easily divisible.

4.   Good money must be durable.

5.   Good money will be relatively small and lightweight compared to its value.

For many years, gold reasonably — though not perfectly — embodied all the above characteristics. Other goods have served as unit of account (shells, cattle, houses, silver), but gold became the most important monetary unit, and in the 17th and 18th centuries gold was synonymous with money. Gold's flaws were that it is relatively heavy, easy to counterfeit, and, were subject to fluctuations in supply. These flaws led to gold's replacement by paper currency backed only by trust that the government would keep its commitment to limit its supply[5].

---

[5] David C Colander, Macroeconomics 4th edition (Mc Graw Hill, Irwin 2001, NY,NY)P 302

Appreciating the value of money

When I look at my three children, I am able to understand and appreciate the value of money as I work to make sure their needs are provided for. To children, however, money seems to grow on trees! Our hard earned money is spent on toys, iPods, cell phones, games, and other fun or pleasurable gadgets. They may have very little appreciation of all the hard labor that goes into earning that money if not educated about this by their parents.

When you really look at it, money represents the combined labor of a chain of people. Individuals and companies buy and sell the services of labor, capital, land, and entrepreneurship in resource markets. For these resources, service companies and individuals pay income to individuals and companies, wages for labor services, interest for capital, rents for the use of the land, and profits for entrepreneurship. This effort generates value. We normally focus on the end product, the car that has been manufactured, or the pig or sheep that has been reared; but we need to realize that much effort in the form of labor, capital and skill have gone into the production of the commodities or end products. Herein is the creation of value.

So we need to learn to appreciate money for what it represents, the combined efforts of many people acting as individuals or companies. From a Biblical perspective this effort represents a labor of love in the service of God for the benefit of society. Money should not therefore be coveted but appreciated. As Christians we must see money for what it represents — an unbroken chain of love leading back to the Father[6].

Tool or resource

Is money a tool or a resource? It's both. It's a tool given by God, something to be used not glorified, appreciated but not elevated[7]. A recent influential paper argued that the straightforward interpretation of money is that it works like a tool, in that it enables the owner to get what he wants. The only difference is that tools are usually specific to a job. I recently attended an introductory course on

[6] Robert Fraser, Marketplace Christianity (New Grid Publishing. Kansas 2006) P 68

[7] Robert Fraser, Marketplace Christianity (New Grid Publishing. Kansas 2006) P66

plumbing and all the tools, the wrench, the socket set, and the pipe cutter were all specific to that particular job. Money does not have this specific quality. Instead, it is more like a resource than a tool per se, a resource which can be used as a store of value and unit of exchange, serving to bring about efficiency within markets.

Master or Servant

Sir Francis Bacon once said, "Money is a good servant but a terrible master." We must always remember that money is a servant and we are to learn to master it. If we allow money to control and master us then it will eventually destroy us so we must be very careful never to let this equation become reversed.

Further, it must be clarified that money itself is not the issue. It is the value we put on it and how we allow it to define who we are and why we do in life what we do. The Bible says that it is the love of money that is the root to all kinds of evil (1 Timothy 6:10).

Jesus the Christ recognized the importance of money and its proper use in the parable of the talents in the Matthew 25:14-30. These verses tell the story of servants who received talents from their master. Two of the servants were wise stewards of the talents and invested them, gaining more from what they had been given and were appropriately rewarded. However, one servant instead of using his master's talents buried it in the ground. In the end, he lost that talent and his reward. The parable of the talents can be confusing if we don't know what a talent is. After all, a talent is no longer used, so we should ask, "What was a talent, anyway?" An ancient talent is best defined as a measure of money. One talent had the value of 6,000 denarii, with one denarius being the equivalent of a day's wages to a common laborer. Doing the math, a talent was worth nearly 20 years of wages to a common laborer during this particular ancient era. Jesus Christ used this valuable money measure to graphically represent the valuable physical and spiritual gifts that God gives to us his people. A monetary talent represents a personal talent, for purposes of this parable of the talents.

In modern English, a "talent" has come to refer to intelligence, skills, aptitudes, and physical abilities that a person possesses. For clarity, and spiritual application, we can further this by saying a talent refers to the time on earth you are given by God, your physical and mental talents and abilities, your spiritual gifts, your energies, personality, experiences, attitudes, and last but not least, your material resources. The principle here is that all we have really belongs to the Master, God, and how we use our talents will determine our rewards. These talents are inclusive of all the details of our lives — time, money, relationships and gifts (spiritual and natural). All we possess is by the grace of God. As wise stewards of our talents we must always seek to glorify God in how we use them. We can do so as we learn how to "master" money and use it not only to improve our current circumstances but to help others and to benefit society. As successful coach Bob Proctor, once said that we must start to see money as an obedient, diligent servant, that we can employ to earn more money, and that we can use it to provide services far beyond the service we, by ourselves, could ever physically provide[8].

---

[8] Bob Proctor, You were born rich (Life Productions 1997) P19.

Use it or lose it

Money only has value if it's being used. That's what makes it useful. The book of Ecclesiastes, part of the wisdom literature of the Bible, addresses this issue in Chapter 5.

"[11] As goods increase, so do those who consume them. And what benefit are they to the owners except to feast their eyes on them? ... [13] I have seen a grievous evil under the sun: wealth hoarded to the harm of its owners." (Ecclesiastes 5:11, 13 NIV)

The message is clear: money is not meant to be hoarded or hidden away. It is meant to be used, to be enjoyed, and to be circulated. This does not mean that we must not save. When we have more money than we need for ordinary expenses, we are wise to save some for later use. The Bible speaks well of the saver noting that the ant wisely stores up food for winter (See Proverbs Chapter 6:6-11). But hoarding is something completely different.

Hoarding comes from a person trying to safeguard against "not having enough," which ultimately—ironically—creates the experience of not having enough.

Hoarding = a belief in "not enough"

The perception that there is never enough to go around drives you to accumulate more and more. In the end, however, this kind of focus ends up creating the state of lack a person is aiming to avoid. Not only will you attempt to store away as much money as you can, you will also resist spending, even on things you really need, and this habit will eventually create a pool of stagnation. If the stagnation grows big enough or lasts long enough, you will end up creating a blockage in the flow of money through your life and your belief that there is not enough money will be proven true.

Money only has value when it is in circulation and making money is an otherwise pointless exercise if you have no plans of using it. Sounds simple, but many people are not aware of this principle and have sacrificed the quality of their lives on the altar of the false belief that there is not enough.

I will always remember the story of old Mr. Chapman, the miser. He used to go around the streets looking for junk that others had discarded so that he could sell it for whatever he could get. Mr. Chapman lived the same way until he died. Because he had no close relatives and friends nearby, the authorities took over his property and the stock of all he had left behind. Imagine the surprise of the policeman rummaging the place to find boxes and boxes of cash amounting to more than $100,000 in the house! Mr. Chapman had hoarded lots of money, but, because he'd never used much of this accumulated money on himself or for other people, his cash was as good as the junk he collected. What a sad story.

Creating money out of thin air

Kenneth Galbraith, a noted Keynesian economist who died in 2006, said that the process by which banks create money is so simple that the mind is repelled. How do banks create money? It's actually so simple, it's like magic. The key is to understand why banks don't keep all the money that people place on deposit in their vaults. They lend the money out. This creates bank deposits.

One key to understanding how banks create money is to know that a financial asset can be created "from nothing", as long as an offsetting financial liability is simultaneously created. They create money by issuing loans with the money that people deposit. The bank charges interest on the value of the amount loaned out. This becomes their proceeds from the loan. This is how banks create money by simultaneously creating an offsetting financial liability. They are able to increase their net worth through the interest charged on the loans. The key point, here, is that wealth can be created and is unlimited. Wealth comes from ideas. The chair you are sitting on right now did not always exist. Someone had the idea to make a chair and made it thus creating a new asset. So wealth comes from ideas and your ideas cost nothing, therefore it is possible to make money from nothing.

This book is about learning how to create money and generate wealth, but first we need to look at some money myths, in our next chapter.

Chapter 2

Money Myths

W e've already dealt with one of the biggest myths concerning money which is that money is not important, but there are a myriad of other limiting beliefs prevailing in our time which can stop us from prospering.

All money myths represent potential mental and emotional pitfalls, blockages and agendas that can stand in the way of material prosperity. Why is this so? It's because beliefs have consequences. Our beliefs represent our "worldview" and (beliefs or our worldviews) are more powerful than you can imagine. The Bible underscores the power of belief when it says in Proverbs 23:7 "As a man thinketh in his heart so is he." Basically, this verse   says that what you believe is what you become. In terms of money, if you believe that making money is hard then you will most likely find it hard to make money. If you believe that you are only capable of making so much money, then that's the threshold at which you will more than likely stop. If you believe that your life is a struggle most likely it will be.

The truth about money is that most of what you believe is not true! There are a multitude of money myths that are held as beliefs in our subconscious minds. They have been received or "downloaded" many times from our parents, society, friends, the media, and, yes, the church. These myths or limiting beliefs have been passed- down from generations before us and serve to hinder our wealth potential and financial success. From the list below, which ones seem to "jump out" at you that resonate within, that you have believed. Make a special note of what these are because you are going to have to take steps to get them out of your system.

99 Money myths

1. Money is the source of all evil.

2. Rich people are greedy.

3. Money is not important.

4. I'll save money when I have enough.

5. Having a good job will get me a lot of money.

6. Money corrupts people.

7. Money can be used to buy anything.

8. Rich people don't care about the poor.

9. I have to work very hard to make money.

10. It takes money to make money.

11. Wealth often brings out the worst in people.

12. Wealthy people are not happy.

13. With much wealth simple things lose their pleasure.

14. You have to be born with money to be wealthy.

15. If the economy were better I could be wealthy.

16. Money is a good measure of my success in life.

17. Money burns a hole in your pocket.

18. Money is hard to come by.

19. Money is my security.

20. Money defines my self-worth.

21. More money equals more problems.

22. There's not enough money to go around.

23. Money doesn't grow on trees.

24. Having lots of money is being greedy.

25. It is not spiritual to have money.

26. My prosperity takes away from someone else's prosperity.

27. You have to struggle to survive.

28. Money causes problems.

29. If I have money, I'll just lose it anyway.

30. God must not want me to have money.

31. Money is filthy lucre.

32. If I have money people will just want me for my money.

33. I'm not good with money.

34. It is more spiritual to be poor.

35. I can't save money.

36. Money makes the world go around.

37. If my parents were rich I would have made it.

38. I have to feel guilty for having lots of money.

39. It is too much trouble having money.

40. Rich people get rich by robbing the poor.

41. I'm not worthy of having lots of money.

42. It is bad to want money.

43. It is filthy being rich.

44. I'll never make money.

45. I don't have enough money.

46. God wants us to be poor so that we are not corrupted by riches.

47. Rich people don't get to go to heaven.

48. You have to sell your soul to have money.

49. Making money is pain.

50. Making money is hard.

51. I can't handle having money.

52. I don't know what I'd do if I had money.

53. Money is frustrating.

54. Jobs are hard to come by.

55. I am never going to get ahead.

56. I am broke.

57. I'm stuck.

58. Money is a curse.

59. No matter what I do I wouldn't make money at it.

60. Money will change me for the worse.

61. I don't really want money anyway.

62. Things are too hard.

63. I don't have any money.

64. Jobs suck.

65. Poor people have less to worry about than rich people.

66. I'm poor.

67. I don't know how to make money.

68. Money causes stress.

69. I'm not destined to have money.

70. Money is not for me.

71. It is almost impossible to make a lot of money.

72. If I had a lot of money I'd lose my friends.

73. Money slips through my hands.

74. If you work hard you'll never be rich anyway.

75. Having lots of money allows you to live life to the fullest.

76. In order to be stay wealthy you have to lie a lot.

77. Being wealthy makes you healthy.

78. Spiritual people don't care about money.

79. In order to be wealthy you have to work hard all the time.

80. If you are wealthy you will have to spend all your time in the fear of losing it.

81. You can't sleep when you have a lot of money.

82. Being happy is a function of being able to afford whatever you want.

83. In order to be wealthy you have to sacrifice your health.

84. In order to be wealthy you have to sacrifice your family.

85. In order to be wealthy you have to sacrifice your leisure activities.

86. Financial success is not worth the price.

87. In order to be wealthy you have to cheat and steal.

88. I am a failure.

89. When I receive money some else loses it.

90. I'll never amount to anything.

91. I'll never succeed.

92. It's all about money

93. Money is the source of happiness.

94. There is nothing money can't buy.

95. Money is scarce.

96. The amount that I can spend is determined by what is in my check book.

97. I can't be a millionaire.

98. I won't be able to protect my wealth.

99. Being wealthy will improve your marriage.

Overcoming limiting beliefs

Once we become aware that we are holding negative or limiting beliefs about money we have to get to the work of clearing them out of our minds and forming new and more empowering, abundance-focused beliefs — and it doesn't have to take forever.

This book is about helping you to develop a balanced view of money, and about helping you release and overcome those negative feelings concerning money so that you can learn to attract, create, multiply and keep money. One very powerful way of ridding ourselves of these negative and limiting beliefs about money is to find and replace them with true, more powerful abundant beliefs. Here is a sample of some more powerful, truthful and abundant beliefs.

- The "love of" money is the root of all kinds of evil.

- Money itself is neither good nor evil, money is neutral.

- Money is a resource to be used to make markets more efficient.

- Money is simply a medium of exchange.

- Money is a store of value.

- Having more money enables me to help more people.

- It's not selfish to want more money so that you can help more people and contribute more.

- You can be both spiritual and wealthy.

- Wealth is a mindset.

- Money is time in foldable form.

- If I have an abundance mentality, I will attract more money into my life.

- If I put my money to work for me, I will have more time to spend with my family and others.

- Many rich people are generous.

- God loves rich people too.

- I will love people and use money.

- I will not love money and use people.
- Money is a terrible master but a good servant.
- I can do all things through Christ who gives me strength.
- I respect and appreciate money.
- Money represents a labor of love of a chain of servants leading back to the father.
- Money provides opportunities for growth and development.
- Money enables me to provide and care for my family.
- It's okay for me to have lots of money.
- There is enough money in the universe for everyone.
- I have the ability to acquire wealth.
- I have the ability to protect my wealth.
- I have the ability to multiply wealth.
- People who are wealthy are not smarter or more talented than I am.
- I was born rich because I am blessed with talents from God.
- God is exceedingly wealthy because the earth is His and the fullness thereof.

- Money cannot buy everything.

- Money is not a measure of my success.

- Money is not my security.

- Money does not define my self-worth.

- Wealthy people can enjoy life.

- I will start saving money now.

- I will make money work for me.

- God wants me to prosper.

- Money is not filthy lucre.

- I can make more money.

- I won't sacrifice my health for wealth.

- I won't sacrifice my family for wealth.

- I will not steal, lie, or cheat to become wealthy.

- I am not a failure.

- I am a success.

- I can discipline myself.

- I can master money; It will not rule me.

- I will make money my servant.

- I am not poor.

- I can learn how to make money.

- I am destined to have money.

- I can handle and protect my money.

- Lack of money is not a root of all kinds of evil.
- Money buys food.
- Failure can be a stepping stone to my success.
- I will never, never give up.
- It's more blessed give.
- I must have something to give.
- Money can grow almost anywhere, it depends on where you plant it.
- I don't have to work hard, but I do have to work smart.
- It takes financial intelligence to make money.
- Jesus talked a lot about money and finances so it must be important.
- Money helps me to provide for my own needs and the needs of my family.
- With money I can give and help others in need.
- Making money for yourself takes the burden off those on whom you might otherwise rely.
- Making money is a good thing.

Removing the Sacred Secular division

Where did the idea come from that money is evil? It came from a religious spirit and a mistranslation of a well-known Bible verse. Jesus, well aware of some of the dangers of riches such as greed and independence from God warns us to "Watch out! Be on your guard against all kinds of greed; life does not consist in an abundance of possessions" (Luke 12:15 NIV). Paul's first letter to Timothy gives us reasons to heed Jesus' warning:

"For we brought nothing into the world, and we can take nothing out of it. [8] But if we have food and clothing, we will be content with that. [9] Those who want to get rich fall into temptation and a trap and into many foolish and harmful desires that plunge people into ruin and destruction. [10] For the love of money is a root of all kinds of evil. Some people, eager for money, have wandered from the faith and pierced themselves with many griefs." (1Timothy 6:7-10 NIV)

Here Paul is warning all people, rich and poor alike not to let their money or riches replace God in their lives. He is urging every human individual to have a healthy dependence on God. If we allow money to become the source of our happiness, self-worth, personal power, joy, freedom or anything else, then we are only setting ourselves up for failure and disappointment in the long-term.

God must be our ultimate source, our ultimate provider, as He is the only one who can bring true joy, happiness and fulfillment into our lives. Without this understanding we will succumb to the pressure to create money with an emotional agenda inappropriately riding on it. If we go in this direction we will definitely fail in the long run precisely because the things we truly desire and seek after have little to do with money.

Our money is not our life, and we must be constantly aware of greed, covetousness and wrong values. Jesus says that we CANNOT serve God and mammon. Money, as we have said, is a good servant, but a horrible master. Paul says that the "love of money" NOT money itself, is the source of much of the evil in the world. Money itself is neutral!

It's our attitude to money and how we use it that will cause money to be seen as good or evil. We were tricked into believing in the sacred –secular view of reality. It's called dualism. Dualism is a view of reality that creates a radical, non-biblical separation between the unseen spiritual reality and the earthly related matters pertaining to the so-called natural things. Although we call it dualism, there are really three categories of things — the sacred, the sinful and the secular.

We all know what the sacred things are; they are those things that are holy (the Holy Bible, the Holy Spirit, holy matrimony), those things that belong to God (the Lord's Day, the Lord's table), those things associated in our minds with the spiritual (prayer, going to church, singing worship songs and hymns, reading our Bibles, etc.).

Sinful things are those things that are not holy, evil things that spiritually corrupt a person and that stand opposed to heaven — stealing, lying, cursing, drunkenness, envy and such like. But then there is third category, the secular.

Secular things are called "worldly", but they are not inherently evil and since they are merely material and temporal in nature are considered neutral and of no eternal significance — working, eating, sleeping, education, business, government, looking after the needs of the body and all the other mundane things we have to do on earth.

In the professions: preaching is sacred, prostitution is sinful, and the audit of a company's books of accounts is secular.

In money matters: The Sunday offering is sacred, the lottery is sinful and money in your back pocket is secular.

In food and drink: The wine of the sacrament is sacred, excessive rum drinking is sinful and orange juice is secular.

In the arts: A Christian tract cover illustration is sacred, a nude picture on the cover of Playboy is sinful, and a picture of the Alps or the beach is secular.

In music: The choir's music is sacred, some types of hard rock music may be sinful, and West Indian calypso music is secular.

I guess you see the point. The problem is that the so-called sacred activities make up a small portion of our daily lives. The overwhelming majority of our time is spent doing the mundane things of life. This is the trap of the dualistic mindset and it's a lie. This lie has forced many a man and woman to favor the ascetic approach. Medieval monks and nuns vowed celibacy, poverty, and social withdrawal in an effort to cut themselves off from secular involvement, but this was no solution.

Solving The Problem

The only solution to this false view of life is to accept that "the earth is the Lord's and everything in it" (Psalm 24:1 NIV). For a believer in Christ the effect of Christ's work on the cross is that there is no area of life that is not sacred! Every aspect of our life is to be set apart for God. Yes, as Christians we have a new birth from above, we are to be dead to the elementary principles of the world as it says in Colossians 2:20, but we do not die to the things of which this world consists, the material things of the world, only to the corruption that empowers them.

We know that God declared all things he created in the natural cosmos and universe to be good (Gen 1:10, 12, 18, 21 and 25) and "very good" in   verse 31. Since all the cosmos was polluted by sin, Christ has redeemed all of it — ALL. When the Spirit of Christ empowers us, we can see the created things for what they are — the work of the Creator. With this understanding, the physical things of the world acquire an eternal, spiritual significance when received with thanksgiving and used for God's glory. Instead of being called "filthy lucre," we can see money for what it really is: a resource to be used and to glorify God. In its use - instead of seeing the making of money as a carnal calling, we can see it being used to help others in need and offered to God as a spiritual ministry in our work and business life.

It is also useful to remember that Jesus, when he was here on the earth, worked as skilled carpenter for at least fifteen years of his earthly ministry. Talk about secular work! An employee should do his work faithfully as unto God. The Book of Colossians admonishes: "whatever you do, whether in word or deed, do it all in the name of the Lord Jesus, giving thanks to God the Father through him."(Colossians 3:17NIV).

"All vocations are ordained by God and intrinsically of value. God's kingdom franchise requires workers of all kinds: plumbers, CPAs, salesmen, housewives, and corporate executives. All of them are called to extend the Father's will and the ways of His kingdom into every sphere of life.[9]"

The Bible can validly be used to oversee the real things of life like work, business, economics, government and politics. We must rise up and bring the redeeming truth of the gospel of Christ to bear forcefully upon the marketplace and the larger macro-economic issues of banking, money management, taxation and economics. If preaching and singing can be done to the glory of God, then so can running the marathon, farming, fishing, marketing, writing, governing a nation and looking after its economy and money management.

---

[9] Dennis Peacocke, Doing business God's way (Rebuild, Santa Rosa California 1995) P7.

In the next chapter we will look at some important areas of money management.

Chapter 3

Money Management

Now that we understand what money is and how important it is, we have to look at the issue of money management. If you do not learn how to manage money you will soon discover that money has learnt how to manage you. There is a popular saying that a fool and his money are soon parted and it is true.

One of the keys to good money management is educating yourself and your children about money. You must make a decision and fixed commitment to developing your financial intelligence now. A lot of our schooling in the past was focused on equipping us to get a good job. Our teachers and educators really wanted us to succeed but we were never taught how to manage our own money and how to make money to work for us. This is critically important as the wealth of a nation is determined by the wealth of the individuals in that nation. Thankfully this is changing as leaders and countries start to switch focus to the benefits which can come from focusing on entrepreneurship. Money management is not about money in itself, but about recognizing the fact that God is the ultimate owner of everything and that we are stewards of the resources he provides which, if used properly and wisely, can generate money and create wealth. Godly families will pass on skills of stewardship and character. Economics is about family. The root word for economics is "Oikos"— literally household management. Economic money management then is about the stewardship of God's economic resources and therefore Christianity, without a practical understanding of basic economic money management, is a contradiction in terms. There is a dire need for change. We need to start training our children to be producers not just consumers. We need to teach them how to create value, how to see needs and how to fill them. We need to start teaching our children to see money as a reward for production and a by-product of serving others. We need to teach our children godly character and how to manage resources.

Money management then is about becoming financially intelligent, becoming financially independent, multiplying resources, stewardship, developing character and fiscal responsibility. Jesus wrapped this all up in one parable which can be found in Luke 19. In this parable a nobleman gives his ten servants ten pounds each, with the command to "Occupy" literally, do business until he returns at which time he would find out how much each servant gained by trading. Those who multiplied the resources entrusted to them were told "well done" and given more responsibility while the resources of the servant who did not multiply his resources, his pounds were taken from him.

Developing financial intelligence

Financial intelligence cannot be developed overnight any more than wealth can be developed overnight. It will take time and disciplined effort. The earlier you learn and increase your financial wisdom the less it will cost you. The longer you wait to learn and increase your financial intelligence the more it will cost you because of years of missed opportunities and mistakes made. As you spend time learning and increasing your financial literacy, every day, every week, you are building wealth, and investing in your financial future. You must learn before you can earn. If you want to be truly successful, you must start to invest in yourself to get the knowledge you need, so that as you grow and increase in wisdom you can make wise financial decisions.

A parable of financial intelligence

The parable of the ten minas is a parable of financial intelligence.

"While they were listening to this, he went on to tell them a parable, because he was near Jerusalem and the people thought that the kingdom of God was going to appear at once. 12 He said: A man of noble birth went to a distant country to have himself appointed king and then to return. 13 So he called ten of his servants and gave them ten minas. "Put this money to work," he said, "until I come back." 14 But his subjects hated him and sent a delegation after him to say, "We don't want this man to be our king." 15 He was made king, however, and returned home. Then he sent for the servants to whom he had given the money, in order to find out what they had gained with it. 16 The first one came and said, "Sir, your mina has earned ten more." 17 "Well done, my good servant!" his master replied. "Because you have been trustworthy in a very small matter, take charge of ten cities." 18 The second came and said, "Sir, your mina has earned five more." 19 His master answered, "You take charge of five cities." 20 Then another servant came and said, "Sir, here is your mina; I have kept it laid away in a piece of cloth. 21 I was afraid of you, because you are a hard man. You take out what you did not put in and reap what you did not sow." 22 His master replied, "I will judge you by your own words, you wicked servant! You knew, did you, that I am a hard man, taking out what I did not put in, and reaping what I did not sow? 23 Why then didn't you put my money on deposit, so that when I came back, I could have collected it with interest?" 24 Then he said to those standing by, "Take his mina away from him and give it to the one who has ten minas." 25 "Sir," they said, "he already has ten!" 26 He replied, "I tell you that to everyone who has, more will be given, but as for the one who has nothing, even what he has will be taken away. 27 But those enemies of mine who did not want me to be king over them—bring them here and kill them in front of me.""""

(Luke 19:11-27 NIV)

There are at least five lessons on financial intelligence here.

1. Jesus expected these men, His servants, to have financial intelligence and to gain or profit by trading. The Bible is loaded with financial intelligence advice. For example we are commanded in Proverbs 6:6-8 to go to the ant, to consider her

ways and to be wise. Ants work without an overseer or ruler, are faithful, are persistent in the execution of their duties, share and cooperate with each other for the benefit of the colony, collect their food in the proper seasons and are highly self-motivated and resourceful. We must be like the ant becoming resourceful as we become financially intelligent.

2. Jesus expected these men, His servants, to be financially independent. What Jesus had given to each of them was enough for each individual. Some may have more than others, but it's no good looking at what others have. We need to consider what we have and we have been given enough. Each of us is gifted with various abilities. God expects us to use our gifts, to learn how to become financially independent so that we can adequately support our families. What we have at first may not be very much, but it is enough. Many times money is simply a test of our obedience to God whether we can be faithful in a little before God would bless us with more.

3. Jesus expected these men, His servants, to exercise proper stewardship over the resources entrusted to them. Stewardship is about the management of resources. This management cannot be motivated by fear, greed, or selfishness, but by our love for God and for each other. If we learn how to handle what God has entrusted to us we'll get more, but if we misuse it, then it will be taken away for someone else to handle wisely.

4. Jesus expected from these men, His servants, faithfulness, springing out of a wellspring of godly character. The Bible says that the fear of the Lord is the beginning of knowledge but fools despise wisdom and instruction (Proverbs 1:7). The servant who was faithful in little was handsomely rewarded. And yes, it's true; God does want us to prosper.

"Blessed is the man who does not walk in the counsel of the wicked or stand in the way of sinners or sit in the seat of mockers. 2 But his delight is in the law of the LORD, and on his law he meditates day and night. [3] He is like a tree planted by streams of water, which yields its fruit in season and whose leaf does not wither. Whatever he does prospers." (Psalm 1:1-3 NIV)

5. Jesus expected from these men, His servants, increase or the multiplication of their resources. One servant increased what he was given by 10 pounds, one by 5 pounds and the third showed no increase. This servant was severely reprimanded as "good for nothing". Jesus told him that at least he could have put his money in the bank and gained some interest.

This parable contains many money management principles, but these principles have to be applied in a number of different areas: cash and banks, spending, savings, debt, retirement, insurance and tax planning. Increasing your knowledge in each of these areas is a part of your financial intelligence development.

Cash and Banks

One of the main things every individual or business must do is to maintain a record of cash, (cash and bank balances) and this is very simple matter of "ins" and "outs". Cash is all the currency and coins on hand, plus bank balances and negotiable money orders and checks. A check is a negotiable instrument drawn against deposited funds, to pay a specified amount of money to a specific person upon demand.

Maintaining a checking account is a great help here as you will not remember all your purchases if you operate solely on cash. So a simple check and deposit book will do the trick along with discipline in keeping a faithful record of whatever goes in and out of the bank account.

If you do not know how much you have you will not be able to control your spending. For those of you who firmly believe in using cash instead of checks or credit - and many of you probably do - you will need to keep track of what goes in and out simply by keeping track of your receipts. Checks have the added difficulties that not every retailer accepts personal checks, and the time delay for checks to be deposited by the recipient and the amount to be withdrawn from our account. For those on tight budgets, cash is better because it is immediate.

Example of a simple cash book						
Record of Bank Deposit			Record of Checks Issued			
Date	Dep. Det.	Deposit	Date	Details	Check No.	Bank
Oct 26	1	78.00	Oct 26	Grocer.	1240	263.73
Oct 27	2	324.75	Oct 28	Gas	1241	75.00
Oct 28	3	609.07	Oct 29	Car Insur.	1242	456.47
Oct 29	4	403.53	Oct 29	House Insur.	1243	348.55
			Nov 4	Index LTD	1244	199.96
						1368.71
				Bal. b/d		525.64
		1894.35				1,894.35

Spending

What's the difference between a need and a want?

Your needs are the things you use and require every day such as a place to live, water, electricity, a way to get to work and clothing. Wants are those things you can live without, but would love to have — the fancy car, the expensive cellphone and expensive designer gear. The key to managing your spending is to first distinguish between your wants and your needs and to develop a spending plan.

We live in a materialistic society with people on a never-ending quest for more — more things, more toys, more to buy. TV commercials bombard us every day with emotive ads to lure us into buying the latest gadgets. Still, we must be good stewards of whatever resources we are entrusted with and, therefore, we must make the most of the money we have already earned while gaining more financial intelligence. We must become money earners but we must also be good money spenders.

To be a good spender there are certain things you are going to have to think hard about, for example: how big of a house do you really need and how expensive a car. One of the biggest traps concerning earning more is the desire to spend more. Developing a spending plan will give you greater control over your financial resources. More importantly, following a spending plan will help you live within your means and know whether something you want is affordable. Developing and following a spending plan will help you circumvent impulse buying and spend your money wisely.

Mike Tyson earned over 400 million dollars over his twenty-year boxing career. By 2004, Mike had become such a big spender that he was 38 million dollars in debt, and hadn't yet turned 40 years old. At the height of his popularity and fortune, Mike Tyson owned six mansions, two white Bengal tigers and 110 cars, including garages full of Bentleys, Mercedes and Rolls Royces. According to Bankruptcy court documents Tyson spent the following:

- Nearly 4.5 million on cars and motor cycles
- 3.4 million on clothes and jewelry
- 7.8 million on personal expenses

- $140,000 on 2 Bengal tigers and $125,000 a year for their trainer
- $2 million on a bathtub for his first wife
- $410,000 on a birthday party, and
- $230,000 on cell phones and pagers during a 3 year period from 1995-1997.

There is no question that Mike Tyson took spending habits to new heights, but if we were honest with ourselves, we would all admit that we are influenced by the temptation to spend more especially when we have grown up with little means and less than enough. The way to counter this temptation is through self-discipline, fiscal responsibility and developing a savings plan so that your spending is moderate and not excessive.

Ask yourself:

Is this purchase necessary to live?

Recommendation: Do not purchase unless you can answer honestly with an absolute yes. If you can live without it then do so or at least cut it back.

Saving

Saving is the opposite side of the coin of spending. Whatever we release in cash flow by curbing excessive spending we can save.

To develop a saver's mindset, you must change the way you feel about spending. You must repeatedly remind yourself that the best things in life are free, or nearly so — spending time with your wife, family and friends does not have to be expensive and they provide the best returns. On the other hand, most of the "stuff" we buy becomes unused after a while and doesn't provide much value anyway if it's just sitting in our wall robes. I am not advocating that we turn ourselves into misers, but if we are going to build wealth we must become good savers and develop a lifestyle of saving.

Unless you are a person of independent means, the importance of a regular saving program cannot be underestimated. Most people seem to prefer the trappings and illusion of wealth over the freedom of actual wealth and by this I mean that many people prefer to look wealthy by becoming big spenders instead of big savers. If you are ever going to build wealth the one thing you will definitely have to focus on is accumulating assets. Spending money on assets instead of on consumer goods is good spending. The life cycle of building wealth dictates that early on in the cycle you focus on buying assets so that you have something to grow. The earlier you start the better. For most people that starting point is saving money. So whether you own your own business or work as an employee, you must think of each dollar as vital resource unit which can be saved so that it can multiply, grow, and work for you on your path to financial independence.

Savings Plan

Total Earnings	–	Spending	=
Saving			

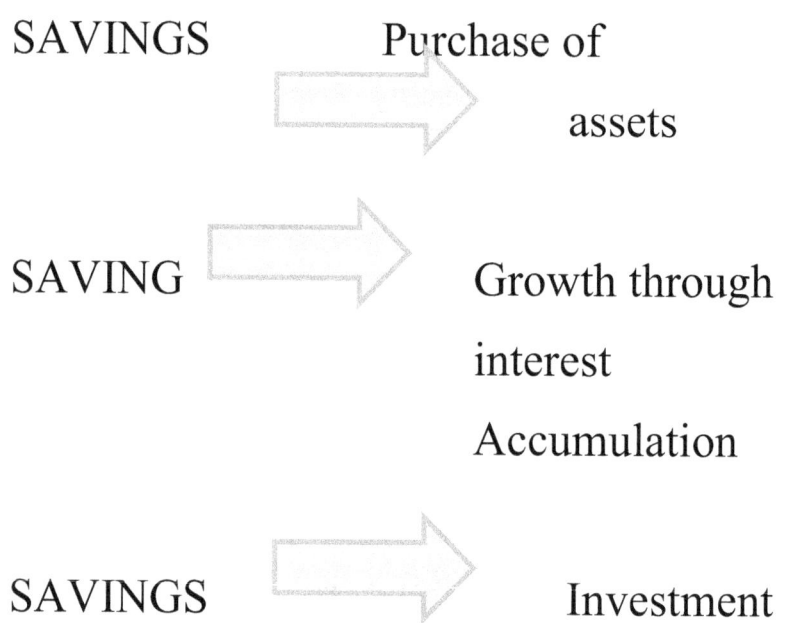

SAVINGS   Purchase of assets

SAVING   Growth through interest Accumulation

SAVINGS   Investment

As your savings grow you will accumulate wealth through the power of compound interest, through the purchase of assets and through investment.

Managing Debt

Solomon wisely perceived that the "rich rule over the poor, and the borrower is servant to the lender" (Proverbs 22:7). This is mainly the result of a lot of consumer debt driven by greedy thoughts and a drive to maintain a certain lifestyle that other people appear to have – the so-called "keeping up with the Joneses". This leads to us purchasing cars, houses, gadgets, etc., that we don't really need, nor can we afford. When we don't have the cash on hand for something, we turn to credit cards or loans. We forget, however, that credit is not cash. It is not money available to spend.

When we have "too much house" or "too much car" and go in over our financial heads to get these things, the money you could be saving goes toward paying off those debts.

But there are kinds of debt that are valuable tools for the financially wise.

Good debt versus Bad debt

The biblically-stated fact that the borrower is servant to the lender does not mean that we should avoid debt like the plague or avoid all debt since not all debt is bad. The Bible never says that it is a sin to borrow. "Neither a borrower nor a lender be" comes not from the Bible but from Shakespeare's *Hamlet*!

Debt only arises when you cannot repay your commitment, for example, when you fail to make payments on your loan commitments.

Bad debt is when you use debt for things that can be consumed or "consumer goods." Credit card debt is often considered bad debt because of the nature of the items that credit cards are used to purchase.

Avoid accumulating debt to purchase everyday items like clothing or food, or vacations or anything else that does not appreciate in value.

Families in financial trouble should avoid using their credit to buy "wants" until they can accumulate savings. Buying "wants" such as television sets, sporting goods or excess furniture should be done on a strictly cash basis. The "saving" of cash will have a stabilizing influence on family finances. Further, families should resolve not to purchase anything on credit until all of their accounts are fully paid. Then, instead of immediately obligating themselves to more payments by purchasing additional items, they should let their savings begin to accumulate.

Good debt is investment debt that creates increased value, for example student loans, real estate loans and business loans that produce wealth in the long run. Steven Silbiger in his book *The Jewish Phenomenon: Seven Keys to the Enduring Wealth of a People* says that the best possible investment you can make in your future is an education. Even if you default on the loan, nobody can take away your education.[10]

In addition, it makes perfect sense if you have, say, a credit card debt of $10,000 at 17% interest to take out a loan at 6% to pay off the credit card. That would be good debt.

Credit Cards

Credit cards that you don't or can't pay off are an example of bad debt, but this does not mean that you cut up all credit cards and never use credit card debt. In fact, in today's sophisticated society, having a credit card is almost essential. I remember travelling once with my family to

---

[10] Steven Silbiger, The Jewish Phenomenon (Longstreet Press, Atlanta Georgia 2000) P 23.

Puerto Rico and it was impossible to rent a car or book a hotel without a credit card.

Many Christian counselors oppose credit cards because they have seen too many people who cannot handle them. However, many people pay off their credit card every month and enjoy the benefit of free interest. This arises from the extra time you have to pay off the credit card. In addition some people get free rewards on their credit card purchases, like a 5% discount on all gas purchased with their credit card, enhanced warranties and consumer protection. In addition, if you pay off your credit card each month on time, you can improve your credit rating. So the key with credit cards is discipline and sensibility.

Retirement

Every single one of us is getting older every day and so it makes sense to start making plans for our retirement. The earlier the better, since social security is not necessarily a sufficient or reliable means of support. In addition, the days of paternalistic employers are over. Retirement planning requires consideration of many components.

Pulling them all together requires careful planning but here are a few strategies:

1. Start immediately. The earlier you start to save the better so you can take advantage of compound interest.

2. Pay yourself first. Establish an automatic savings plan where your money is deducted from your pay before you see it. This makes the process of saving a lot less painful and puts your retirement plan on autopilot.

3. Maximize contributions to tax-deferred plans. If your employer offers a savings match program make sure to save enough to maximize this free money. By contributing to a defined contribution plan, you pay yourself even before the government gets its cut. This is because, in most cases, the money you contribute is tax deductible. This makes it tax deferred though *not* tax free.

4. Focus on owing your own home. Home ownership has been an important wealth building strategy for years. This is because as you pay off your mortgage debt in a disciplined way you will be building your own equity while benefitting from the likely increase in the market value of the property over time.

5. Develop and have a cash reserve. This should be enough to cover 3-6 months of expenses, so that you do not need to dip into your retirement contributions for extra money.

6. Make your money hard to reach. You can do this by adopting a straightforward investment policy. Investing not only increases your wealth through dividends, but also makes it harder for you to spend the money on things. Remember, though, to always seek advice where necessary.

Mortgage Payments

Owing your own home may be a key wealth building strategy, however, one must be aware that the interest component of a mortgage is substantial, and make plans to prepay the mortgage.

In 2002, I took out a 25-year house mortgage of $235,000 at 9% interest. Over a twenty-five-year period my total payments to the mortgage company would have amounted to $591,000. When you take away the principal of $235,000 this amounts to a whopping $356,000 in interest! Today, I do not owe anything for my house—but how? Years ago I discovered that prepaying your mortgage, even by a few dollars per week, can literally save you a fortune. Why? Because any additional payment goes directly to the loan's principal, thus reducing the significant interest charged over the life of the loan. Here's what is saved with extra payments on a 30-year, $100,000, 7% interest rate mortgage.

If the mortgage were not prepaid the total payments would amount to $239,508 and the total interest payments would amount to $139,508. So you see that prepaying your mortgage must be a key strategy in your home ownership, wealth-building plan.

The below financial work up is amazing.

Extra monthly Payment	Total Savings	Years of Loan
$25	$18,214	26.8
$50	$31,654	24.3
$75	$42,097	22.3
$100	$50,507	20.6
$200	$72,695	16.1

I had heard about a prepaying a mortgage, but always thought it had to be in the hundreds of dollars to make a difference, but even $25 a month makes a huge difference.

Taxes

One way to skillfully manage income is through tax savings. There is a difference between tax evasion, which is illegal, and tax avoidance which is legal. Tax avoidance strategies have been used by the wealthy for generations and we can all employ these strategies ourselves to decrease the amount we pay to the government.

Most countries allow pension contributions as a tax deductible expense, so contributions to any pension scheme or defined contribution plan should be maximized. In many countries, mortgage interest is also a tax deductible expense as well as investments in new shares — these should be maximized where possible. Keep in mind, though, that you don't need a mortgage just so you can have the tax deduction. The tax deduction reduces the cost, but it does not turn costs into income. A tax deductible expense is still an expense.

It is also important to know that the tax laws were written in favor of business owners, enabling them to legally avoid paying taxes on items that are generally non-tax deductible for individuals. This means that it is important to consider whether to operate as an individual or to set up a company. When you are a business owner many of the things you already spend money on become tax deductible expenses. These may include things like internet fees and computer costs, cellphone charges, computer supplies, a percentage of utilities, postage and mileage.

Insurance

Should Christians ignore economics and just trust God? I don't think so.

Money management in relation to insurance is a part of the broader concept of risk management. The Bible cautions us against undue worry (Matthew 6:4), but the entire book of Proverbs urges us to manage our affairs intelligently and with wisdom. There is no perfect security in the world but the Bible does say that the wise and prudent man foresees the evil that is coming and prepares himself, but the foolish do not and suffer for it (Proverbs 22:3). Insurance is one of those things that we must understand and use wisely in our "risk management" plans.

In brief, risk management involves identifying what risks you and your family are exposed to and determining how best to manage those risks. Risks include such things as sickness, injury, disability, loss of life, loss or damage to property and personal liability. We need to consider what financial impact these risks would have on our personal estate, personal lives and families. Once these risks are identified, we should try to reduce or eliminate their financial impact by considering what safeguards we can take or put in place. A person may install a burglar alarm system in their house or car. A person may start an exercise program to reduce health risks. Financially speaking, most of the unavoidable financial risks can be transferred to a third party by purchasing insurance.

Life Insurance

Life insurance comes in two basic forms. Term insurance provides "pure protection" where you buy the death benefit or face value of the policy, say $125,000. This provides temporary coverage over a specific period of time stated in the policy - say five, ten, fifteen or twenty years. Employer-provided life insurance is typically term coverage.

Cash-value life insurance, which includes whole life and universal life, provides not only a death benefit, but a savings component as well. A part of your premium goes towards the savings component (called the cash value), where the earnings accumulate but are tax deferred or postponed. You can borrow against the cash value, withdraw it and use it to help pay your premiums, or let it accumulate for your long-term goals such as retirement. The type of life insurance you purchase will depend on your needs.

Term insurance offers the greatest death benefit for the dollar, but the cost of term insurance rises significantly as you age. If your partner is dependent on you, or if your family is dependent on your income to pay the mortgage, to raise the children and to meet ordinary living costs, then life insurance may be essential for your financial plan. It's one sure way to provide financial security for your partner and children if you die.

Generally, the younger you are, or if you are married, the greater the need to have life insurance. The assumption is that when you are older you will need less insurance because you will have accumulated some assets and probably own your own home.

Company insurance

Insurance coverage is a fairly standard cost of doing business. Businesses should investigate insurance coverage for fire and other hazards, legal liability, property and motor vehicles, workers compensation, theft, medical and other employee benefits, life and disability and business interruption. The small business proprietor should consider taking out a "key man" insurance policy which can be a form of protection for his family if he dies prematurely.

Having insurance often provides a false sense of security and it is more important to have the *right* coverage than to just have coverage. It is important to understand the type of coverage your business needs and has, and to read and understand the fine print in all policies. It is important to reevaluate your business insurance needs periodically.

The following types of insurance coverage should be discussed with your insurance agent:

- Product Liability – protects you if your product causes injury to the consumer.

- General Liability – provides coverage for legal defense and financial compensation and is designed to protect the business from claims filed by third parties.

- Property insurance – protects the business against physical damage or loss from such incidents as fire and theft.

- Basic Fire insurance – protects the business from fire.

- Theft insurance – protects the business in the event of theft.

- Employer's liability – protects the business if someone is injured, whether or not the business was at fault.

- Workers compensation – protects the business if employees are hurt on the job.

- Business interruption – compensates the business for loss of income if the business has to vacate its premises due to a disaster that causes the business to totally or partially suspend operations.

- Vandalism & malicious damage – protects the business in the event of vandalism and related crimes.
- Vehicle insurance – provides protection for the automobiles used or owned by the business.

Now it is time to learn about riches and how to be truly rich, which is our next chapter.

Chapter 4

True Riches

To discover what true riches are we are going to look at the parable of the shrewd manager.

The Parable of true riches

Jesus told his disciples:

"There was a rich man whose manager was accused of wasting his possessions. 2 So he called him in and asked him, 'What is this I hear about you? Give an account of your management, because you cannot be manager any longer.' 3 'The manager said to himself, "What shall I do now? My master is taking away my job. I'm not strong enough to dig, and I'm ashamed to beg-- 4 I know what I'll do so that, when I lose my job here, people will welcome me into their houses." 5 So he called in each one of his master's debtors. He asked the first, "How much do you owe my master?" 6 "Eight hundred gallons of olive oil," he replied. The manager told him, "Take your bill, sit down quickly, and make it four hundred." 7 Then he asked the second, "And how much do you owe?" "A thousand bushels of wheat," he replied. He told him, "Take your bill and make it eight hundred." 8 The master commended the dishonest manager because he had acted shrewdly. For the people of this world are more shrewd in dealing with their own kind than are the people of the light. 9 I tell you, use worldly wealth to gain friends for yourselves, so that when it is gone, you will be welcomed into eternal dwellings. 10 Whoever can be trusted with very little can also be trusted with much, and whoever is dishonest with very little will also be dishonest with much. 11 So if you have not been trustworthy in handling worldly wealth, who will trust you with true riches? 12 And if you have not been trustworthy with someone else's property, who will give you property of your own?

13 No servant can serve two masters. Either he will hate the one and love the other, or he will be devoted to the one and despise the other. You cannot serve both God and Money. 14 The Pharisees, who loved money, heard all this and were sneering at Jesus. 15 He said to them, 'you are the ones who justify yourselves in the eyes of men, but God knows your hearts. What is highly valued among men is detestable in God's sight.'"

(Luke 16:1-15 NIV)

This chapter from the book of Luke is about discovering what true riches are. Jesus teaches us that there are two types of riches. Most people are after earthly riches without first understanding the purpose of money or riches. In fact, we need to make a distinction between money, riches and wealth for they are not the same, although they are related and the words are often used interchangeably. This chapter we will devote to riches, while wealth will be dealt within the next chapter.

We have already looked at money in chapter 1. We saw that money was simply a resource, a tool which facilitates efficiency in trading in markets. Money has certain key characteristics, is divisible into smaller units, durable and transportable. Money acts as a medium of exchange and a store of value.

So what are riches? The Greek word for riches used in the above parable means abounding or abundant.

So riches refer to an abundance of money or possessions.

This is the same meaning attached to the Hebrew word for rich used of Abraham in Genesis 13:2.

"And Abraham was very rich in cattle, in silver and in gold."

The word used here for rich means heavy or laden. So worldly riches relates to an abundance of money and possessions; whether these possessions be stocks, bonds, or other investments, houses or lands — the point is abundance.

The desire for riches

We live in a consumer-driven materialistic society on a never-ending search for significance in things that can never truly satisfy. We buy the latest plasma TV, the fastest or most expensive car, the biggest house, the latest cellphone or other stuff to satisfy ourselves.

When we rely on material possessions to feel a sense of satisfaction then we have set ourselves up for certain failure and long-term disappointment. The desire and drive to acquire, consume and possess more and more physical resources as an end in itself leads towards insecurity and lack of fulfillment. This is because as Jesus says, a man's life does not consist of the abundance of the things he possesses (Luke 12:15). This verse does not say that there is anything wrong with possessions just that our possessions do not define who we are. 1Timothy 6:17 says that God created all things for us to enjoy. So being rich should be a matter of thanksgiving, not pride. Every possession that a person can possibly own comes from the creator,   (Psalm 24:1). So riches can rightly be counted as a blessing from God. It was in this spirit that

King David declared in 1 Chronicles 29:12: "Both riches and honor come from thee." Nowhere, then, does the Bible says that having possessions and becoming rich are wrong in themselves.

The deception of riches

However, Jesus did warn that riches could keep a person out of the kingdom.

> "How hard it is for the rich to enter the kingdom of God."
>
> (Mark 10:23 NIV).

Affluence, he taught, can destroy peace (Matthew 6:24), hinder people from seeing to the needs of others (Luke 16:19-31), stand between individuals and the gateway to eternal life (Mark 10:17-27) and even serve to bring God's judgment (Luke 12:16-21). Jesus was teaching us of the un-profitableness of riches without God.

In verse 11 of Luke 16, Jesus indicates that true riches are more desirable than the abundance of things. Our riches and our money are actually given to us as tests as to who will be trusted with true riches. Obviously, from what

Jesus said in verse 13, everyone must choose for themselves whether they will serve God or serve themselves by worshipping money and possessions. Obviously, God wants us to choose Him and to seek first the kingdom. We must be careful, therefore, not to be like the ungodly and turns our possessions into idols, things that we strive to live for, as this will surely demonstrate that we do not really believe in the one and only Living God.

"The idols of the nations are silver and gold, made by the hands of men. 16 They have mouths, but cannot speak, eyes, but they cannot see; 17 they have ears, but cannot hear, nor is there breath in their mouths. 18 Those who make them will be like them, and so will all who trust in them."
(Psalm 135:15-18 NIV)

"4 But their idols are silver and gold, made by the hands of men. 5 They have mouths, but cannot speak, eyes, but they cannot see; 6 they have ears, but cannot hear, noses, but they cannot smell; 7 they have hands, but cannot feel, feet, but they cannot walk; nor can they utter a sound with their throats. 8 Those who make them will be like them, and so will all who trust in them."

(Psalm 115:4- 8 NIV)

It's important, therefore, to note the following:

1. Our possessions and money may buy companionship, but they cannot buy love.
2. Our possessions and money may buy a house, but cannot buy a home.
3. Our possessions and money may buy a bed, but cannot buy rest.
4. Our possessions and money may buy thrills, but not true satisfaction.
5. Our possessions and money may be able to buy us food and doctors, but cannot guarantee us health.

Money and possessions cannot give us biological children of our own, peace of mind and freedom from fear and worry. Nor can they provide protection from every possible calamity. But everything that money, possessions and the abundance of riches cannot do, GOD CAN do, and

God is constantly warning us against us putting our trust in these things.

Severe Warnings

God's warnings against us putting our trust and confidence in riches are for good reason. Only God is fully dependable. There were many times in history when the possessions people trusted in, proved worthless. The Bible warns of a time coming when all of our earthly riches will fail.

> "Wealth is worthless in the day of wrath, but righteousness delivers from death."
> (Proverbs 11:4 NIV)

This is a severe warning. There is coming a day of wrath, a day of God's judgment, a day of final accounting. The prophet Zephaniah echoes:

> "14 The great day of the LORD is near — near and coming quickly. Listen! The cry on the day of the

LORD will be bitter, the shouting of the warrior there. 15 That day will be a day of wrath, a day of distress and anguish, a day of trouble and ruin, a day of darkness and gloom, a day of clouds and blackness, 16 a day of trumpet and battle cry against the fortified cities and against the corner towers. 17 I will bring distress on the people and they will walk like blind men, because they have sinned against the LORD. Their blood will be poured out like dust and their entrails like filth. 18 Neither their silver nor their gold will be able to save them on the day of the LORD's wrath. In the fire of His jealousy the whole world will be consumed, for He will make a sudden end of all who live in the earth."

(Zephaniah 1:14-18 NIV).

There are similar warnings against the deceitfulness of riches in the New Testament:

"1 Now listen, you rich people, weep and wail because of the misery that is coming upon you. 2 Your wealth has rotted, and moths have eaten your clothes. 3 Your gold and silver are corroded. Their corrosion will testify against you and eat your flesh like fire. You have hoarded wealth in the last days." (James 5:1-3 NIV)

"15 Do not love the world or anything in the world. If anyone loves the world, the love of the Father is not in him. 16 For everything in the world—the cravings of sinful man, the lust of his eyes and the boasting of what he has and does—comes not from the Father but from the world. 17 The world and its desires pass away, but the man who does the will of God lives forever."
(1 John 2: 15-17 NIV)

God's warnings are for everyone to recognize His goodness and to put their trust in Him not in the abundance of things. Therefore, whether we have an abundance of worldly possessions or not, we must first of all put our trust in God. We need to view worldly riches as a precious gift from God to provide for our families, neighbors and the world. The message of Biblical prosperity is a precious blessing which more and more Christians are learning to walk in.

However, while the Bible does teach of God's desire to bless and prosper us, He also expects us to be good stewards of with what he entrusts to us. A message of Biblical prosperity and abundance does not give us a license to be greedy or materialistic, but to be rich towards God.

The truly rich man

It is important for us to understand Christ's teaching in the parable of Luke chapter 16 if we are ever going to learn how to manage and deal with worldly riches, and it is absolutely clear from the parable that this is what Jesus wants us to be able to do.

Before we can learn how to handle worldly riches we must first understand that the rich man in the parable is God. God is a God of abundance.. God never runs out of anything. There is nothing about God that smacks of insufficiency, lack or limit. God didn't just create our planet He created the eight others that make up the solar system. Our sun is a star and there is an estimated 100 billion more stars in our galaxy—that's 100,000,000,000 stars. Yes, God is a god of relentless abundance. He wasn't content with one planet, one solar system or even one galaxy, for the realm of His created order is too vast for any human mind to fully comprehend.

God has created our little planet Earth with an incredible amount of richness. There are vast natural resources that lie under the earth's surface such as minerals and oil. God gave us plants and trees that produce after their own kind. We have animals on the ground, birds in the air, creatures in the sea and the sun in the sky. There is no doubt that it was part of God's plan for man always to have abundant provision, but for what purpose?

The purpose of worldly riches

The purpose of worldly riches is so that we can be rich towards God. Anyone who has an abundance of worldly riches and is not rich towards God is a fool.

We find such a fool in Luke Chapter 12. Jesus is speaking.

"15 'Watch out! Be on your guard against all kinds of greed; a man's life does not consist in the abundance of his possessions.' 16 And he told them this parable: 'The ground of a certain rich man produced a good crop. 17 He thought to himself, "What shall I do? I have no place to store my crops." 18 Then he said, "This is what I'll do. I will tear down my barns and build bigger ones, and there I will store all my grain and my goods. 19 And I'll say to myself, 'You have plenty of good things laid up for many years. Take life easy; eat, drink and be merry.'" 20 But God said to him, "You fool! This very night your life will be demanded from you. Then who will get what you have prepared for yourself?" 21 This is how it will be with anyone who stores up things for himself, but is not rich toward God."

(Luke 12:15-21 NIV)

There are many people in the world today who have an abundance of riches yet are extremely poor! And there are many people who think that they are poor, but they are so rich! The real issue is not how much you have but how you use your resources not only for yourselves but for others, for the advancement of the kingdom of God, for the defense of the poor and the fatherless.

"1 God presides in the great assembly; he gives judgment among the 'gods': 2 How long will you defend the unjust and show partiality to the wicked? 3 Defend the cause of the weak and fatherless; maintain the rights of the poor and oppressed. 4 Rescue the weak and needy; deliver them from the hand of the wicked."
(Psalm 82:1-3 NIV).

True riches

True riches have nothing to do with what you have.
True riches have nothing to do with how much money you own.
Being truly rich has nothing to do with what or whom you control.

True riches are not denominated in earthly currency, but in heavenly currency!

"19 Do not store up for yourselves treasures on earth, where moth and rust destroy, and where thieves break in and steal. 20 But store up for yourselves treasures in heaven, where moth and rust do not destroy, and where thieves do not break in and steal. 21 For where your treasure is, there your heart will be also."
(Matthew 6:19-20 NIV).

How is it possible to convert our early riches to heavenly? Jesus tells us.

"Sell your possessions and give to the poor. Provide purses for yourselves that will not wear out, a treasure in heaven that will not be exhausted, where no thief comes near and no moth destroys."
(Luke 12:33 NIV).

It is hard to understand this radical teaching of Jesus except by the Holy Spirit, but the most fundamental assumption we must have in the handling of money or riches is that we are not the owner, only a steward. This is very hard for us to accept. We think that we have worked so hard to acquire what we believe to be our own and we believe that we have the right to do with it as we please. God says, no. We are stewards and must learn to exercise proper stewardship.

So how do we convert our early currency to heavenly currency? We convert our earthly resources to the currency of heaven when we use our resources not only for ourselves, but to bless others and to sow into the kingdom of God as instructed by the Lord. It's important to note that not all giving is directed by God.

Much giving is done out of fear, compulsion and guilt. The fact is that we have a lot of resources which can be used for the kingdom. Worldly wealth is not limited to money and possessions. We were all born rich! God expects each of us to share our time, talents, knowledge, experience, and skills for the benefit of others. Our problem is our selfishness.

> *There are so many*
> *resources available and we*
> *are not the least bit aware*
> *of what can be used as*
> *heavenly currency — our*
> *smiling face, warm heart,*
> *listening ears,*

> *Money doesn't change men, it merely*
> *unmasks them. If a man is naturally selfish*
> *or arrogant or greedy, the money brings*
> *that out, that's all.*
> *Henry Ford*

We need Jesus to deliver us from the spirit of selfishness. This world is filled with people who are in need. God is concerned about the poor, the lost, the least and the last. He wants us to be his hands extended right where we are now as we can see in Matthew chapter 25.

"35 For I was hungry and you gave me something to eat, I was thirsty and you gave me something to drink, I was a stranger and you invited me in, 36 I needed clothes and you clothed me, I was sick and you looked after me, I was in prison and you came to visit me. 37 Then the righteous will answer him, 'Lord, when did we see you hungry and feed you, or thirsty and give you something to drink? 38 When did we see you a stranger and invite you in or needing clothes and clothe you? 39 When did we see you sick or in prison and go to visit you?' 40 The King will reply, 'I tell you the truth, whatever you did for one of the least of these brothers of mine, you did for me.' 41 Then he will say to those on his left, 'Depart from me, you who are cursed, into the eternal fire prepared for the devil and his angels. 42

For I was hungry and you gave me nothing to eat, I was thirsty and you gave me nothing to drink, 43 I was a stranger and you did not invite me in, I needed clothes and you did not clothe me, I was sick and in prison and you did not look after me.' 44 They also will answer, 'Lord, when did we see you hungry or thirsty or a stranger or needing clothes or sick or in prison, and did not help you?' 45 He will reply, 'I tell you the truth, whatever you did not do for one of the least of these, you did not do for me.' 46 Then they will go away to eternal punishment, but the righteous to eternal life."

(Matthew 25:35-46 NIV).

The passage also tells us that in the last day, and in the final analysis, each of us will have to stand before God and give an account of our stewardship of that which was another man's property. We will all be held accountable for how we have used our earthly riches. Those who have been wise, faithful and careful will be greatly rewarded.

Principles of stewardship

As long as we live in the world, we cannot separate ourselves completely from dealing with money and material goods. This was never God's intention and it should not be ours. The real question is, how are we using our resources and abundance for God's good purposes?

God wants each of us to be wise investors and good managers. If we fail, God will dismiss us just like the unjust steward was fired in the parable of Luke chapter 16 and find someone else who whom he can trust and who he can use. To be successful we need to understand and accept the underlying basis of God's biblical stewardship which is that:

- God owns all things because he created all things.
- We own nothing. All we have comes from God.
- We owe God thanks because Jesus paid fully for our indebtedness at Calvary.
- It is more blessed to give than to receive. (Acts 20:35)

- We can look to God to supply all of our material needs when we really trust Him, believe His word and seek first the kingdom of God.

"22 Then Jesus said to his disciples: 'Therefore I tell you, do not worry about your life, what you will eat; or about your body, what you will wear. 23 Life is more than food, and the body more than clothes. 24 Consider the ravens: They do not sow or reap, they have no storeroom or barn; yet God feeds them. And how much more valuable you are than birds! 25 Who of you by worrying can add a single hour to his life? 26 Since you cannot do this very little thing, why do you worry about the rest? 27 Consider how the lilies grow. They do not labor or spin. Yet I tell you, not even Solomon in all his splendor was dressed like one of these. 28 If that is how God clothes the grass of the field, which is here today, and tomorrow is thrown into the fire, how much more will he clothe you, O you of little faith! 29 And do not set your heart on what you will eat or drink; do not worry about it. 30 For the pagan world runs after all such things, and your Father knows that you need them. 31 But seek his kingdom, and these things will be given to you as well. 32 Do not be afraid, little flock, for your Father has been pleased to give you the kingdom."

(Luke 12: 22-32 NIV)

Biblical stewardship has nothing to do with the church's annual stewardship service, but much more to do with our understanding that God owns everything and our need to be careful and faithful as we depend on Him for everything.

How we handle money and other resources is the "litmus test" of our stewardship and true character. A litmus test is a test in which a single factor is decisive in proving the presence or absence of something like how we test for chlorine in a pool. God's litmus test will tell whether in this life we were rich towards God or whether we served mammon.

Now it is time to learn not only how to be rich towards God, but how to be wealthy which is in our next chapter.

Chapter 5

True Wealth

Perhaps the best place to start is to look at some of the ideas people have about wealth and about being wealthy.

Understanding wealth

Being wealthy is:

- Having a lot of money in the bank, let's say over one million dollars.
- Being debt free.
- Owning a dream house, car or other luxury items you cannot afford right now.

- Not having to work for a boss.
- Financial independence.
- Being a part of an elite group of people like the "fortune 500 Club".
- Having everything you want.
- Being loved by family and friends.
- Having tangible assets to meet the physical needs of yourself and love ones.
- Having a balanced life.
- Inner peace and spiritual enlightenment.
- Excellent health and freedom from disease.
- All of the above.

So it all comes back down to how we are going to define wealth. We have to be able to "pin it down" and get our hands around it.

Accountants define wealth as assets minus liabilities, but in today's volatile financial world, assets can quickly become liabilities if we are not careful. It is said that eighty percent of America's wealth exists on paper. In the previous chapter, we established that money was different from riches and that riches and wealth are not the same thing. The scriptures speak extensively of money, riches and wealth — three related but distinct concepts. So let's look again at the definitions.

Money is simply a resource used to simplify trading. Money gives us the right to the goods and services of others.

Riches refer to the abundance of resources be that money or possessions, whether those possessions be stocks, bonds, houses, lands or other investments.

Wealth, on the other hand, is multi-dimensional.

I like Robert Fraser's definition of wealth given in his book, *Market Place Christianity*, best: Wealth refers to the ability to create money by controlling the means of production. The Bible often associates wealth with land and cattle, which in a modern economy equates to business which is the modern means of production. If money were water, then riches would be buckets of it and wealth a river of water. Or, in terms of cash, riches are a pile of cash and wealth is cash flow. Riches are limited and can be depleted by loss or consumption. Wealth on the other hand, creates a steady flow of income. [11]

The first time the Bible mentions someone with a lot of money, it speaks of a righteous man, Abraham (His name was Abram first), and he was very rich.

"And Abram was very rich in cattle, in silver, and in gold."
(Genesis 13:2 KJV)

Not only was Abraham rich, he was also wealthy.

"Abram had become very wealthy in livestock and in silver and in gold." (Genesis 13:2 NIV)

Abraham's servant says about him in Genesis 24:35:

"And the LORD hath blessed my master greatly; and he is become great: and he hath

---

11 Robert Fraser, Marketplace Christianity (New Grid Publishing 2006) P68.

given him flocks, and herds, and silver, and gold, and menservants, and maidservants, and camels, and asses."

According to Genesis 12:1, Abraham's wealth included:

- Livestock, food and commodities for trade (flock, cattle and herd).
- Money (silver and gold)
- Employees (male and female servants)
- Transportation fleets (camels and donkeys)
- Land.

So Abraham was not only rich, he was wealthy. According to the Oxford Advance Learners dictionary wealth is "the state of being rich." It is possible to have an abundance of material possessions and yet not be wealthy!

Dimensions of wealth

Wealth is multi-dimensional. First wealth is a blessing from God.

Wealth as a blessing from God

All wealth comes from God and belongs to God. The creation is God's wealth and that creation included us, the most precious part of God's creation.

> [3] Then God said, "Let there be light," and there was light. [4] And God saw that the light was good. Then he separated the light from the darkness. [5] God called the light "day" and the darkness "night."
>
> And evening passed and morning came, marking the first day.
>
> [6] Then God said, "Let there be a space between the waters, to separate the waters of the heavens from the waters of the earth." [7] And that is what happened. God made this space to separate the waters of the earth from the waters of the heavens. [8] God called the space "sky."
>
> And evening passed and morning came, marking the second day.

⁹ Then God said, "Let the waters beneath the sky flow together into one place, so dry ground may appear." And that is what happened. ¹⁰ God called the dry ground "land" and the waters "seas." And God saw that it was good. ¹¹ Then God said, "Let the land sprout with vegetation— every sort of seed-bearing plant, and trees that grow seed-bearing fruit. These seeds will then produce the kinds of plants and trees from which they came." And that is what happened. ¹² The land produced vegetation—all sorts of seed-bearing plants, and trees with seed-bearing fruit. Their seeds produced plants and trees of the same kind. And God saw that it was good.

¹³ And evening passed and morning came, marking the third day.

¹⁴ Then God said, "Let lights appear in the sky to separate the day from the night. Let them be signs to mark the seasons, days, and years. ¹⁵ Let these lights in the sky shine down on the earth." And that is what happened. ¹⁶ God made two great lights—the larger one to govern the day,

and the smaller one to govern the night. He also made the stars. ¹⁷ God set these lights in the sky to light the earth, ¹⁸ to govern the day and night, and to separate the light from the darkness. And God saw that it was good.

¹⁹ And evening passed and morning came, marking the fourth day.

²⁰ Then God said, "Let the waters swarm with fish and other life. Let the skies be filled with birds of every kind." ²¹ So God created great sea creatures and every living thing that scurries and swarms in the water, and every sort of bird— each producing offspring of the same kind. And God saw that it was good. ²² Then God blessed them, saying, "Be fruitful and multiply. Let the fish fill the seas, and let the birds multiply on the earth."

²³ And evening passed and morning came, marking the fifth day.

²⁴ Then God said, "Let the earth produce every sort of animal, each producing offspring of the same kind—livestock, small animals that scurry

along the ground, and wild animals." And that is what happened. [25] God made all sorts of wild animals, livestock, and small animals, each able to produce offspring of the same kind. And God saw that it was good.

(Genesis 1:3-25 NLT)

"For all the animals of the forest are mine,
and I own the cattle on a thousand hills.
[11] I know every bird on the mountains,
and all the animals of the field are mine.

(Psalm 50:10-11 NLT)

"The earth is the Lord's, and everything in it.
The world and all its people belong to him.
[2] For he laid the earth's foundation on the seas
and built it on the ocean depths."

(Psalm 24:1-2 NLT)

[8] The silver is mine, and the gold is mine, says the Lord of Heaven's Armies

(Haggai 2:8 NLT)

All of creation belongs to God. It is all His.

But why did God choose to create? God chose to create because he is creative and because he is a God of love. Love needs someone to be the object of that love. So God created man to share his life and love with.

"26 And God said, 'Let us make man in our image, after our likeness: and let them have dominion over the fish of the sea, and over the fowl of the air, and over the cattle, and over all the earth, and over every creeping thing that creeps upon the earth.' 27So God created man in his own image, in the image of God created he him; male and female created he them." (Genesis 1:26-27 KJV)

The creation story teaches us much about God and about ourselves.

1.   We learn about God.
    ➢ We learn that God is creative.
    ➢ We learn that God is distinct from his creation.

- We learn that God owns all things, the gold, the silver, the minerals and animals are all his.
- We learn that God is in ultimate control of his creation and the world.

2. We learn about ourselves.

- We learn that we are valuable to God who created us.
- We learn that we are given a place above the animals.
- We learn that we have been made caretakers of all God's vast mineral and animal wealth.

"And God blessed them, and God said unto them, 'Be fruitful, and multiply, and replenish the earth, and subdue it: and have dominion over the fish of the sea, and over the fowl of the air, and over every living thing that moves upon the earth.'"
(Genesis 1:28 KJV)

We, the human race, were born into a wealthy universe, and placed upon an earth full of rich resources. We have to accept, therefore, that God is the God of wealth, of abundance, of riches and diversity. Wealth, therefore, is a precious gift from God, and we were created to share God's wealth and to use it for the advancement of His kingdom and the development of nations.

There is no doubt that there are many challenges to experiencing wealth and many dangers associated with the acquisition of wealth and riches. However, because there are enemies in our way seeking to stop us from obtaining our rightful inheritance does not change the fact that God intends for us, His children, to have access to the wealthy resources of the planet. It's our right, but as we will see later, it is also a great responsibility.

Productive versus Consumptive view of wealth

"Be fruitful, and multiply, and replenish the earth, and subdue it: and have dominion over the fish of the sea, and over the fowl of the air, and over every living thing that moves upon the earth."

(Genesis 1:28 KJV)

God's original intent was for humans to be entrepreneurial and to produce whatever they needed for existing and prospering in the earth.

Every human being has it in his genes to be productive. The earth itself was designed by God to be productive. Anyone who desires progress in life must learn to operate the law of productivity. Our lives must yield fruit. The question is: How do you get fruit? And the answer is: You get it from the seed. How do you get the seed? You get it from God. [12]

"Now He who supplies seed to the sower and bread for food will supply and multiply your seed for sowing and increase the harvest of your righteousness" (2 Corinthians 9:10 NASB)

God has placed within every individual a compelling drive to produce, to be successful, and He has done this not

---

[12] Dr. Mensa Otabil, Four Laws of Productivity, the International Central Gospel Church, Ghana 1991 P25.

only by giving us the original creation mandate, but the ability.

> "And you shall remember the Lord your God, for *it is* He who gives you power to get wealth, that He may establish His covenant which He swore to your fathers, as *it is* this day."
>
> (Deuteronomy 8:18 NKJV)

The New International version says "the ability to produce wealth."

The ability to produce wealth comes from God. He gives us the desire, the ability and the power. It's a part of God's creative ability and ours. Our wealth comes from the inside. Each of us has a seed. Each seed is of a different variety and you have to discover what that seed is. For some, the seed may be your intellect, the ideas that God gives you. For others, it may be the abilities of your hands, and the many talents you have which you have to put to productive use.

> "Poor is he who works with a negligent hand, But the hand of the diligent makes rich."

(Proverbs 10:4 NASB)

So each of us was born wealthy, we just need to discover that wealth and thank God for the limitless human imagination, creative brains and ingenious hands. We may well discover that we are wealthier than we think!

Our consumer driven western-style societies have given us a one-sided non-Biblical consumptive view of wealth. But God expects us to not just be consumers but producers. We are to create things for others instead of expecting others to create things for us. We have the God given ability in us to find new ways of seeing things and of doing things. As we do this, we will start to see that we can produce wealth for it is more important for us to be able to produce wealth than to possess it. Robert Fraser says that wealth gives us the ability to provide for others without depleting our resources. For example, if a needy family had arrived on Abram's doorstep, he could have taken care of them by putting them to work in his field (business). But instead of costing Abram , they would have expanded his production capabilities. Wealth, therefore, gives us the ability to create a spiritual oasis.[13] We can hire good people and take good care of them and good care of our customers through the production of goods and services. This is why business is so important in wealth creation.

Relational wealth

God's original intent was not only for humans to be entrepreneurial but relational. We do need each other and our relatives and friends are an important part of our wealth.

Our children are a part of that wealth.

"How blessed is everyone who fears the LORD,
Who   walks   in   His   ways.
When you shall eat of the fruit of your hands,
you will be happy and it will be well with you.
Your   wife   shall   be   like   a   fruitful   vine
within   your   house,

---

[13] Marketplace Christianity by Robert Fraser, New Grid Publishing, KS 2006 P.69

your   children   like   olive   plants
around   your   table.
Behold, for thus shall the man be blessed
who fears the LORD. The LORD bless you from
Zion,
And may you see the prosperity of Jerusalem all the
days   of   your   life.
Indeed, may you see your children's children.
(Psalm 128:1-6 NASB).

Your wife is a precious gift from God made especially for
you!

"He who finds a wife finds a good thing and obtains
favor from the LORD." (Proverbs 18:22 NASB)

One man was overhead to say, "If my wife is from God
I would not like to see what a gift from the devil would be
like!" There is hope for this man and his marriage as God
can turn anything around.

"House and wealth are an inheritance from fathers, but a prudent wife is from the LORD." (Proverbs 19:14 NASB)

I thank God for my wife, Yolanda, my best friend and confidante, a treasure greater than rubies.

"An excellent wife, who can find?
For her worth is far above jewels.
The heart of her husband trusts in her,
and he will have no lack of gain.
She does him good and not evil
all the days of her life."
(Proverbs 31:10-12).

Below is a picture of my wife and I with our daughter Rickeda on her twentieth birthday. This year in November we will be celebrating twenty five years of marriage. An excellent wife I have truly found and I give God thanks.

Likewise your children are precious gifts from God and a part of your divine inheritance. They are like arrows in the hand of a warrior.

> "Behold, children are a gift of the LORD,
> The fruit of the womb is a reward.
> Like arrows in the hand of a warrior,
> so are the children of one's youth.
> How blessed is the man whose quiver is full of them."

(Psalm 127:3-5 NASB)

In my quiver are Delandro, Daniel and Rickeda —
three of the best children you could ask for and who
love me, their father!

The picture below is of the Taylor family in 2009 at my
eldest son's graduation.

My three children are all unique.

Daniel the youngest is the quiet one, simple but
resourceful.

Rickeda the middle one and only girl is the born leader,
strong but very loving and like most women,
resourceful.

Delandro the eldest, is the creative genius, the graphic
designer par excellence who lives in the visual world of
the picture that paints a thousand words.

What would life be like without trusted friends? So your trusted friends and especially those who provide you with wise counsel are part of your relational wealth.

"Oil and perfume make the heart glad,
So a man's counsel is sweet to his friend."
(Proverbs 27:9-10 NASB).

So too your brothers and sisters in Christ with whom God has united you.

"Behold, how good and how pleasant it is
For brothers to dwell together in unity!
It is like the precious oil upon the head,
Coming down upon the beard,
Even Aaron's beard,
coming down upon the edge of his robes.
It is like the dew of Hermon
Coming down upon the mountains of Zion;
For there the LORD commanded the blessing—
life forever."
(Psalm 133:1-3 NASB).

Below is a picture of longtime friend Michael Riggs and his wife Denie from Alabama on the island of Cariacou in the Grenadines.

The truth is that there are many things that material wealth and riches cannot buy. Money may be able to pay for many doctors, but it cannot guarantee our health. Money can buy us many houses, but cannot make a house a home. A man's material wealth will certainly attract many women, but a prudent and faithful wife is from the Lord. A man may be able have many children, but a loving and godly family comes as a blessing from God. Truly much wealth is denominated in the relationships we have with our family and friends. Within this community of life and love, we learn that we need each other and that there is always a place, or someone to protect and support us in times of hardship. Nothing is more tragic than the man whose only friend is his wallet. Like Old Mr. Chapman, this man will end up going to his grave isolated and lonely. This man may be feared, but likely not loved and respected. Building, nurturing and cherishing relationships with other people is a part of building true wealth.

Multi-generational wealth

Since wealth is a blessing from God, wealth is, therefore, good. Wealth is one of God's means of providing for us, his children. These simple statements are important and point to the most important agency through which God's wealth is distributed, the family. Every nation's prosperity is based on its view and care of the family.

"The Lord had said to Abram, "Leave your native country, your relatives, and your father's family, and go to the land that I will show you. ² I will make you into a great nation. I will bless you and make you famous, and you will be a blessing to others. ³ I will bless those who bless you and curse those who treat you with contempt. All the families on earth will be blessed through you."

(Genesis 12:1-3 NLT)

This covenant of blessing was committed by God to Abraham and his family, his seed. We see it first being realized in Abraham's son Isaac:

"A severe famine now struck the land, as had happened before in Abraham's time. So Isaac moved to Gerar, where Abimelech, king of the Philistines, lived.

² The Lord appeared to Isaac and said, "Do not go down to Egypt, but do as I tell you. ³ Live here as a foreigner in this land, and I will be with you and bless you. I hereby confirm that I will give all these lands to you and your descendants, just as I solemnly promised Abraham, your father. ⁴ I will cause your descendants to become as numerous as

the stars of the sky, and I will give them all these lands. And through your descendants all the nations of the earth will be blessed. [5] I will do this because Abraham listened to me and obeyed all my requirements, commands, decrees, and instructions."
(Genesis 26:1-5 NLT)

Because of Abraham's faithfulness Isaac his son inherited the blessing:

"When Isaac planted his crops that year, he harvested a hundred times more grain than he planted, for the Lord blessed him. [13] He became a very rich man, and his wealth continued to grow. [14] He acquired so many flocks of sheep and goats, herds of cattle, and servants that the Philistines became jealous of him"
(Genesis 26:12-14 NLT)

Isaac sowed in the land and reaped a hundredfold. The principle of investing, involves the law of sowing and reaping: there is no reaping without first sowing. To activate multi- generational wealth, we first have to learn how to sow and how to persevere through adversity.

"Now all the wells which his father's servants had dug in the days of Abraham his father, the Philistines stopped up by filling them with earth. [16] Then Abimelech said to Isaac, 'Go away from us, for you are too powerful for us.' [17] And Isaac departed from there and camped in the valley of Gerar, and settled there. [18] Then Isaac dug again the wells of water which had been dug in the days of his father Abraham, for the Philistines had stopped them up after the death of Abraham; and he gave them the same names which his father had given them. [19] But when Isaac's servants dug in the valley and found there a well of flowing water, [20] the herdsmen of Gerar quarrelled with the herdsmen of Isaac, saying, "The water is ours!" So he named the well Esek, because they contended with him. [21] Then they dug another well, and they quarrelled over it too, so he named it Sitnah. [22] He moved away from there and dug another well, and they did not quarrel over it; so he named it Rehoboth, for he said, "at last the LORD has made room for us, and we will be fruitful in the land."

(Genesis 26:15-22 NASB)

Isaac called the next well "Esek" meaning controversy and the next well "Sitnah" meaning opposition, but nothing could stop this man of God.

And he called the next well Rehoboth because, as he said, God had made room for him. Rehoboth means a place of enlargement and flourishing. Isaac's servants had dug two wells before Rehoboth and the herdsmen of Gerar quarreled with Isaac's herdsmen. So when they dug the third well and there were no quarrels, Isaac named it Rehoboth saying, "Now the Lord has given us room and we will flourish in the land."

The generational transfer of wealth then flowed through Jacob.

> Then Jacob took fresh rods of poplar and almond and plane trees, and peeled white stripes in them, exposing the white which *was* in the rods. [38] He set the rods which he had peeled in front of the flocks in the gutters, *even* in the watering troughs, where the flocks came to drink; and they mated when they came to drink. [39] So the flocks mated by the rods,

and the flocks brought forth striped, speckled, and spotted. [40] Jacob separated the lambs, and made the flocks face toward the striped and all the black in the flock of Laban; and he put his own herds apart, and did not put them with Laban's flock. [41] Moreover, whenever the stronger of the flock were mating, Jacob would place the rods in the sight of the flock in the gutters, so that they might mate by the rods; [42] but when the flock was feeble, he did not put *them* in; so the feebler were Laban's and the stronger Jacob's. [43] So the man became exceedingly prosperous, and had large flocks and female and male servants and camels and donkeys.

(Genesis 30:37-43 NASB)

Abraham, Isaac and now Jacob. That's three generations. Relational wealth is multi-generational and it's oriented towards the long run not the short run.

"Now that Jacob had returned from Paddan-aram, God appeared to him again at Bethel. God blessed him, [10] saying, "Your name is Jacob, but you will not be called Jacob any longer. From now on your name will be Israel."[a] So God renamed him Israel.

^{11} Then God said, "I am El-Shaddai—'God Almighty.' Be fruitful and multiply. You will become a great nation, even many nations. Kings will be among your descendants! ^{12} And I will give you the land I once gave to Abraham and Isaac. Yes, I will give it to you and your descendants after you." (Genesis 35:9-12 NLT)

God chose Abraham as the father of the faithful because He knew that Abraham could be trusted to impart everything he knew to the next generation.

"For I have chosen him, so that he may command his children and his household after him to keep the way of the LORD by doing righteousness and justice, so that the LORD may bring upon Abraham what He has spoken about him." (Genesis 18:19 NASB).

This is an important lesson for us as parents. We must teach our children and impart all that God has given us to them, so that our wealth — spiritual, material, and social — can be passed on down through the generations. We can only do this by teaching them the truth, boldness and faith in God to move mountains and to walk in prophetic destiny. We have to, through faith, destroying all false philosophies and mindsets which are intended to take our children captive so that they do not possess their rightful inheritance promised through Abraham.

We must pass our faith on to our children.

"A good man leaves an inheritance to his children's children."
(Proverbs 13:22 NASB).

Godly families will also pass on the skills of stewardship and character as a primary guarantee of success. They don't emphasize things or money. Any man who wants his business to remain successful for generations to come, and stay in the hands of the family, must train his children to take over the business.

They must understand the spirit that brings success: a long-term vision, care for people and relationship building, and an overall understanding that they are stewards accountable to God for how they handle everything he gives them.

The reason that God gives us power to get wealth is based on God's promise to Abraham that his seed would possess the earth and be heirs of the world based on the righteousness of faith. It is only by this faith that we become Abraham's seed and heirs according to God's promise...

> "For the promise to Abraham or to his descendants that he would be heir of the world was not through the Law, but through the righteousness of faith." (Romans 4:13 NASB)

...and through faith belong to Christ.

> "And if you belong to Christ, then you are Abraham's descendants, heirs according to promise." (Galatians 3:29 NASB)

We believe that God wants to raise up Christian dynasties, families who teach their children from one generation to the next and build a snowball of wealth to use for the kingdom. But this will only happen as God's people learn, by disciplined practice of managing of private property, to be good stewards.[14]

---

[14] Dennis Peacocke, Doing business God's way, Rebuild Santa Rosa California 1995, P38

The wealth of nations

Not only is the wealth that God gives us the ability to create a multi-generational inheritance, it is also for the national good and progress. God has an inheritance in all the nations and His promise to Abraham was not only to bless his seed, but to bless all nations. All nations are blessed with an abundance of wealth. We can define wealth in this regard as the total natural and human resources which a country contains or owns.

However, the truth is that there are many "poor" nations. These are nations that have lots of wealth in terms of natural resources, but for decades their populations have struggled to make ends meet. A county can have a lot of gold and diamonds like Guyana here in the Caribbean yet struggle to create wealthy conditions for its citizens. Many other countries are blessed with natural resources — gold and diamonds, bauxite, crude oil and cocoa — and yet struggle to create the conditions necessary for its citizens to prosper. Globalization and the current global recession have all presented severe challenges to many small developing nations to make ends meet. Lack of skills, knowledge and abilities all play a part in the presence or absence of wealth development. The specter of war, crime and violence, and systematic global corruption has all played a part in perpetrating systematic poverty in the earth. However God's desire is to bless the nations but the nations must see their need for God and cry out to him.

This is what Israel did when they were in the bondage of Egypt. They cried out to God and He delivered them. When the children of Israel left Egypt God gave them great favor so that they went out of Egypt with great wealth. God wanted this people, this new nation to be wealthy. He told them that He did not want them to borrow from the other nations because he was well able to take care of them. He told them that he had made a covenant with them and that this covenant involved giving them the power to produce wealth and to prosper.

"But you shall remember the LORD your God, for it is He who is giving you power to make wealth that He may confirm His covenant which He swore to your fathers, as *it is* this day."

(Deuteronomy 8:18 NASB)

But God also gave them strict warnings lest the nation take His grace, love and prosperity for granted, and forget him.

"For the LORD your God is bringing you into a good land, a land of brooks of water, of fountains and springs, flowing forth in valleys and hills; ⁸ a land of wheat and barley, of vines and fig trees and pomegranates, a land of olive oil and honey; ⁹ a land where you will eat food without scarcity, in which you will not lack anything; a land whose stones are iron, and out of whose hills you can dig copper. ¹⁰ When you have eaten and are satisfied, you shall bless the LORD your God for the good land which He has given you.

¹¹ "Beware that you do not forget the LORD your God by not keeping His commandments and His ordinances and His statutes which I am commanding

you today; [12] otherwise, when you have eaten and are satisfied, and have built good houses and lived *in them*, [13] and when your herds and your flocks multiply, and your silver and gold multiply, and all that you have multiplies, [14] then your heart will become proud and you will forget the LORD your God who brought you out from the land of Egypt, out of the house of slavery. [15] He led you through the great and terrible wilderness, *with its* fiery serpents and scorpions and thirsty ground where there was no water; He brought water for you out of the rock of flint. [16] In the wilderness He fed you manna which your fathers did not know, that He might humble you and that He might test you, to do good for you in the end. [17] Otherwise, you may say in your heart, 'My power and the strength of my hand made me this wealth'."
(Deuteronomy 8:7-18 NASB).

Could it be that many nations are not prospering because they have failed to remember God or have rejected Him altogether? Could it be that the nations have forgotten that it is God who gives the power to get wealth? God is anxious to bless the nations for the nations are His inheritance.

"Arise, O God, judge the earth! For it is you who possesses all the nations." (Psalm 8:2 NASB)

"Arise, O God, judge the earth: for thou shalt inherit all nations."
(Psalm 82:8 KJV).

And God has promised that if His people will humble themselves and pray and seek His face and turn from their wicked ways He will do just that.

" 13 If I shut up the heavens so that there is no rain, or if I command the locust to devour the land, or if I send pestilence among My people, 14 and My people who are called by My name humble themselves and pray and seek My face and turn from their wicked ways, then I will hear from heaven, will forgive their sin and will heal their land."
(2 Chronicles 7:13-14 NASB)

So let us heed God's instruction to pray, intercede and fast for God to heal the land and bless the nations.

The wealth of humanity

True wealth is more than money and things. True wealth is based on a relationship with God the Father through his son Jesus Christ. Without this relationship, all men are deceived into thinking of themselves as wealthy when in reality they are poor, destitute and naked.

> You say, 'I am rich. I have everything I want. I don't need a thing!' And you don't realize that you are wretched and miserable and poor and blind and naked. [18] So I advise you to buy gold from me—gold that has been purified by fire. Then you will be rich. Also buy white garments from me so you will not be shamed by your nakedness, and ointment for your eyes so you will be able to see. [19] I correct and discipline everyone I love. So be diligent and turn from your indifference.

²⁰ "Look! I stand at the door and knock. If you hear my voice and open the door, I will come in, and we will share a meal together as friends. (Revelation 3:17-20 NLT)

"And what do you benefit if you gain the whole world but lose your own soul?" (Matthew 16:26 NLT)

Can it be any clearer? The most important thing in life is not things, it's not possessions; it's a relationship with God through His son Jesus Christ and Christ alone. This is because Jesus was God's only answer for the ills of human society.

" 16 For God so loved the world that He gave His only begotten Son, that whoever believes in Him shall not perish, but have eternal life. 17 For God did not send the Son into the world to judge the world, but that the world might be saved through Him. 18 He who believes in Him is not judged; he who does not believe has been judged already, because he has not believed in the name of the only begotten Son of God."

(John 3:16-18 NASB).

The Bible from Genesis to Revelation covers a wide range and includes a vast amount of matter, but it has one all-governing and conclusive objective. God has one and only one purpose. And what is the one single comprehensive purpose? The answer is Christ![15]

Although Judaism and the law originated with God, the enemy used it to distract mankind from God's eternal purpose in Christ and it was even used to crucify the Son of God. Jesus came to set us free from the "curse of the law" so that we can enjoy the benefit of a wealthy relationship with his Son Jesus Christ and to know the "unsearchable riches of Christ" (Ephesians 3:8).

"You know the generous grace of our Lord Jesus Christ. Though he was rich, yet for your sakes He

---

[15] T. Austin Sparks, The purpose of God, www.austin-sparks.net/english/000417.html

became poor, so that by His poverty He could make you rich."

(2 Corinthians 8:9 NLT)

No matter how much money you have, if you don't see reality according to God's word, you are poor. Relational peace with God brings freedom from debilitating sin and envy. How many rich people do you know who are debilitated by alcoholism, drugs, lust, or envy? They're not wealthy. They may be rich but they're not wealthy.[16]

Wealth begins with personal peace with God. Jesus puts it this way:

"The kingdom of heaven is like a treasure hidden in the field, which a man found and hid again; and from joy over it he goes and sells all that he has and buys that field." (Matthew 13:44 NASB)

---

[16] Dennis Peacocke, Doing Business God's Way, Rebuild Santa Rosa California 1995, P45.

To inherit the kingdom and gain eternal life is worth more than anything one can imagine. It's worth giving up everything for. Again, what does it profit a man to gain the whole world and lose his own soul? The scriptures speak of something or someone being God's treasure — God's people. We are God's treasure.

> "But you are *a chosen race*, A royal *priesthood, a holy nation, a people for God's own possession.*"
> (1 Peter 2:9 NASB).

This verse is a reference to God's covenant with his people which was first established with the people of Israel which is recorded in the book of Exodus.

> " 5 Now then, if you will indeed obey My voice and keep My covenant, then you shall be My own possession among all the peoples, for all the earth is Mine; 6 and you shall be to Me a kingdom of priests and a holy nation." (Exodus 19:5-6 NASB)

In the above Exodus passage, the conditions of the covenant were hearing God's voice and keeping the covenant by entering into relationship with God and remaining in that relationship. The same principle applies to the passage in 1 Peter although no conditions are stated because the conditions have been fully met in Christ! We are God's treasure, God's possession, and God desires that every soul be in a wealthy relationship with him. He does not want us to live our lives for ourselves and then be lost.

"Behold, all souls are mine." (Ezekiel 18:4 NASB)

"The person who sins will die." (Ezekiel 18:20 NASB)

But God has no pleasure in the death of the wicked.

"Do I have any pleasure in the death of the wicked, declares the Lord GOD, rather than that he should turn from his ways and live?"
(Ezekiel 18:23 NASB)

For God is not willing that any should perish.

> "The Lord is not slow about His promise, as some count slowness, but is patient toward you, not wishing for any to perish but for all to come to repentance."
> (2 Peter 3:9 NASB)

This means that God wants all men to come to repentance, to confess their sin and to call upon him for salvation, deliverance and healing. This is the only way to enter God's kingdom and become a part of God's treasure through a relationship with Jesus Christ, God's only begotten Son. Together all Christians are God's treasure chest and individually His jewels, his most valuable and precious possession.

Let's review the various dimensions of wealth:

- Wealth is blessing from God.
- Wealth is derived from our productive efforts.
- Wealth is denominated in our earthly relationships.

- Wealth is transferred through the family to successive generations.

- Wealth is denominated in our relationship with God through His Son Jesus Christ.

God wants us to be wealthy, to enjoy a wealthy relationship with Him, to enjoy the wealth of His rich abundant resources, and to utilize them for our good. God wants us to enjoy wealthy relationships with each other and to enjoy individual and national success. This journey to success comes with great responsibility.

The responsibility that comes with wealth

Many people pray and ask God for riches and great wealth but how many are able to carry the burden of that responsibility?

"From everyone who has been given much, much will be required; and to whom they entrusted much, of him they will ask all the more."
(Luke 12:48 NASB)

The responsibility that comes with wealth is faithful stewardship as caretakers of what God has placed in our hands.

"In this case, moreover, it is required of stewards that one be found trustworthy." (1 Corinthians 4:2 NASB)

" 10 He who is faithful in a very little thing is faithful also in much; and he who is unrighteous in a very little thing is unrighteous also in much. 11 Therefore if you have not been faithful in the use of unrighteous wealth, who will entrust the true riches to you? 12 And if you have not been faithful in the use of that which is another's, who will give you that which is your own?"
(Luke 6:10-12 NASB)

God is, therefore, looking for integrity of character, a servant's heart, in those with whom He will entrust with the riches of His resources and the wealth of His creation.

Our characters will be tested as Abraham's and as Joseph's were.

God called Abraham to sacrifice his only son and he was prepared to do so and obey God because he trusted God's word. After Abraham had passed the test, God pronounced a great blessing on Abraham and his seed.

> "By Myself I have sworn, declares the LORD, because you have done this thing and have not withheld your son, your only son, 17 indeed I will greatly bless you, and I will greatly multiply your seed as the stars of the heavens and as the sand which is on the seashore; and your seed shall possess the gate of their enemies."
> (Genesis 22:16-17 NASB)

Joseph, too, in the book of Genesis, displayed the kind of character and responsibility that comes with being a faithful and trustworthy steward. Joseph's character was severely tested. He literally went from the pit to the prison before God promoted him to the palace. When he was a young teenager, his brothers sold him as a slave into

Egypt. His master Potiphar discovered that he was a capable and trustworthy person and put him in charge of everything in his household. In the course of time, Joseph was misunderstood, lied upon, and put in prison for a crime he did not commit. However, Joseph did not lose his sense of loyalty to God and sense of stewardship. While in prison, the warden recognized Joseph's qualities and made him overseer, responsible for everything that was done there. Joseph had passed the test of impeccable character and godly servant-hood. Later, Joseph would become the prime minister of Egypt and carry an even greater responsibility.

" 38 Then Pharaoh said to his servants, 'Can we find a man like this, in whom is a divine spirit?' 39 So Pharaoh said to Joseph, 'Since God has informed you of all this, there is no one so discerning and wise as you are. 40 You shall be over my house, and according to your command all my people shall do homage; only in the throne I will be greater than you.' 41 Pharaoh said to Joseph, 'See, I have set you over all the land of Egypt.' 42 Then Pharaoh took off his signet ring from his hand and put it on Joseph's hand, and clothed him in garments of fine linen and put the gold necklace around his neck. 43 He had him ride in his second chariot; and they proclaimed before him, 'Bow the knee!' And he set him over all the land of Egypt. 44 Moreover, Pharaoh said to Joseph, 'Though I am Pharaoh, yet without your permission no one shall raise his hand or foot in all the land of Egypt."

(Genesis 41:38-44 NASB)

Not only was Joseph able to make the king very rich from this position of responsibility, but he was able to save many lives, including that of his family members during the severe famine that lasted for more than seven years.

As we accept the responsibility, as we pass God's tests to demonstrate our faithfulness with little, God will entrust us with more resources. As we accept the responsibility, God will break the poverty mindset that we have inherited from our past.

Breaking the poverty mindset

To break the poverty mindset we have to switch to a mindset of abundance.

One of the models of economics is called the scarcity model of economics. Economics, we are told, is about the study of scarce resources. In truth, there are two different ways of seeing the world: the scarcity model and the abundance model. As a Christian and citizen of the kingdom of heaven, I no longer believe everything that I was taught at university. Scarcity may be a fundamental economic problem of seemingly unlimited human needs and wants in a world of seemingly limited resources. Economists assert that we have insufficient productive resources to fulfill all human needs and wants. However in the kingdom of God there is no scarcity and no lack! Hallelujah!

" 13 For the LORD has chosen Zion; He has desired it for His habitation. 14 This is my resting place forever; here I will dwell, for I have desired it. 15 I will abundantly bless her provision; I will satisfy her needy with bread."

(Psalm 132:13-15 NASB).

There is always enough provision and that's why the Lord has taught us to pray:

"Our Father who is in heaven,

Hallowed be your name.

10 Your kingdom come.

Your will be done,

On earth as it is in heaven.

11 Give us this day our daily bread."

(Matthew 6:9-11 NASB)

There will always be enough bread, enough of God's provision, and enough deliverance from the poverty mindset. The poverty mindset is a mindset of lack. It says that there is a finite economic pie and that for us to prosper someone else has to lose, but this is not true as God's resources are unlimited. Jesus demonstrated this when He was on the earth when he turned the water into wine for the guests at the wedding banquet.

The poverty mindset releases a powerful consumptive spirit which benefits the rich and impoverishes the poor. It leads to much impulse buying, excessive debt, financial crisis and mismanagement. The poverty mindset tells people to pursue money without creating value. Work is given a dirty label. Gambling, the lottery and theft are efforts to make money without creating value.[17] The apostle Paul spoke about this poverty spirit:

> "But those who want to get rich fall into temptation and a snare and many foolish and harmful desires which plunge men into ruin and destruction. 10 For the love of money is a root of all sorts of evil, and some by longing for it have wandered away from the faith and pierced themselves with many griefs."
> (1 Timothy 6:9-10 NASB)

It's the love of money which is the root of all kinds of evil not money itself and both the rich and the poor fall prey to this disease. The Bible is clear that poverty is the

---

[17] Robert Fraser, Marketplace Christianity (New Grid Publishing, KS 2006) P.74-75

result of our poor choices which trap us in a cycle of slavery to money. Consider the following quotes from the wisdom of the Proverbs:

"An inheritance gained hurriedly at the beginning will not be blessed in the end."
(Proverbs 20:21 NASB)

"Poverty and shame will come to him, who neglects discipline, but he who regards reproof will be honored."
(Proverbs 13:18 NASB)

"Laziness casts into a deep sleep, and an idle man will suffer hunger." (Proverbs 19:15 NASB)

"The plans of the diligent lead surely to advantage, but everyone who is hasty comes surely to poverty. 6 The acquisition of treasures by a lying tongue is a fleeting vapor, the pursuit of death."
(Proverbs 21:5-6 NASB)

"A man who wanders from the way of understanding will rest in the assembly of the dead. 17 He who loves pleasure will become a poor man; He who loves wine and oil will not become rich." (Proverbs 21:16-17 NASB)

There is precious treasure and oil in the dwelling of the wise, but a foolish man swallows it up." (Proverbs 21:20 NASB)

"The desire of the sluggard puts him to death, for his hands refuse to work." (Proverbs 21:25 NASB)

"Do not be with heavy drinkers of wine, Or with gluttonous eaters of meat; 21 For the heavy drinker and the glutton will come to poverty, And drowsiness will clothe one with rags." (Proverbs 23:20-21 NASB)

"He who tills his land will have plenty of food, but he who follows empty pursuits will have poverty in plenty. 20 A faithful man will abound with blessings, but he who makes haste to be rich will not go unpunished. 21 To show partiality is not good, because for a piece of bread a man will transgress. 22 A man with an evil eye hastens after wealth and does not know that want will come upon him." (Proverbs 28:19-22)

A get-rich-quick mentality, indiscipline, dishonesty and laziness bring poverty whilst diligence, wisdom and hard or smart work bring plenty.

We must therefore resist and reject the idea so prevalent in the Christianity of the past, that to be poor is spiritual. Yes, we must guard ourselves against the deceitfulness of riches and the traps which are associated with the handling of material wealth, but this does not mean that God does not want us overcome the poverty mindset and make the transition from scarcity to abundance. This we will do as we enter into the kingdom of God.

The wealthy mindset

A wealthy mindset comes when we accept that God is a god of wealth and limitless abundance, the owner and maker of everything, and the only one who is able to do whatever he pleases.

"Now to Him who is able to do far more abundantly beyond all that we ask or think, according to the power that works within us."
(Ephesians 3:20 NASB)

"The heavens are yours; the earth also is yours; the world and all it contains, you have founded them."
(Psalm 89:11 NASB)

"But our God is in the heavens; He does whatever He pleases."
(Psalm 115:3 NASB)

In the past, God chose to shower his blessings on Israel His chosen.

"39 *Then He brought them out with silver and gold,* and among His tribes there was not one who stumbled. 38 Egypt was glad when they departed, for the dread of them had fallen upon them. 39 He spread a cloud for a covering, and fire to illumine by night. 40They asked, and He brought quail, and satisfied them with the bread of heaven. 41 He opened the rock and water flowed out; It ran in the dry places like a river. 42 For He remembered His holy word with Abraham His servant; 43 And He brought forth His people with joy, His chosen ones with a joyful shout. 44 He gave them also the lands of the nations, that they might take possession of the fruit of the peoples' labor, 45 to that they might keep His statutes and observe His laws."
(Psalm 105:38-45 NASB)

And he has chosen to do it for us his covenant people and righteous seed.

"The righteous man will flourish like the palm tree, he will grow like a cedar in Lebanon. 13 Planted in the house of the LORD, *they will flourish in the courts of our God.* 14 They will still yield fruit in old age; They shall be full of sap and very green, 15 to declare that the LORD is upright; He is my rock, and there is no unrighteousness in Him."
(Psalm 92:12-15 NASB)

"Let our sons in their youth be as grown-up plants, and our daughters as corner pillars fashioned as for a palace; 13 Let our garners be full, furnishing every kind of produce, and our flocks bring forth thousands and ten thousands in our fields; 14 Let our cattle bear without mishap and without loss, let there be no outcry in our streets! 15 How blessed are the people who are so situated; *How blessed are the people whose God is the LORD!"*
(Psalm 144:12-15 NASB)

And to bring us into a wealthy place.

"We went through fire and through water, yet You brought us out **into a place of abundance."**
(Psalm 66:12 NASB)

"You visit the earth and cause it to overflow;

You greatly enrich it;

The stream of God is full of water;

You prepare their grain, for thus You prepare the earth.

10 You water its furrows abundantly,

You settle its ridges,

You soften it with showers,

You bless its growth.

11 You have crowned the year with Your bounty,

And Your paths drip with fatness.

12 The pastures of the wilderness drip,

And the hills gird themselves with rejoicing.

13 The meadows are clothed with flocks

And the valleys are covered with grain;

They shout for joy, yes, they sing."

(Psalm 65:9-13 NASB)

> "Thou hast caused men to ride over our heads; we went through fire and through water: but thou brought us out **into a _wealthy place_**."
> (Psalm 66:12 KJV)

When we have arrived at the wealthy place, this is the wealthy mindset. The wealthy mindset does not come from watching movies like "the Secret", or by simply changing your limiting beliefs about wealth. The wealthy mindset comes from understanding that God will only do for you what He can do through you; you become a conduit through which God can release His blessing. At the same time, the wealthy mindset understands that God's abundance does not apply only to finances, but to the emotional, physical and spiritual dimensions of life as well.

> "Beloved, I pray that in all respects you may prosper and be in good health, just as your soul prospers." (3 John 1:2 NASB)

With a wealthy mindset comes the ability to be the solution and answer to many of the world's ills, business and other social problems. As we trust God to give us the wisdom and the solutions, God will give us great favor so that we can advance His kingdom. The person with the wealthy mindset will:

- Always be looking for and finding new ways of doing things as circumstances are always changing.
- Be a producer and not just a consumer always seeking to create new things and to be innovative.
- Always be looking for new improvements, never accepting things as they are.
- Always be willing to try new things, to find his/her own answers, even if it means "going against the grain".
- Never be afraid of failure but see failure as an opportunity to learn rather than as an embarrassing mistake to avoid.
- Be risk takers, not allowing fear to stop them from moving forward.

While a rich man may be making others poor while making himself rich, a wealthy man creates riches or income for others and his systems maintain the supply of abundance. A wealthy man perceives a product, creates a factory to produce the product, and employs others to work in it thereby changing the lives of others, enhancing their community and nation.

So, as we allow God to bring us to the wealthy place, with a wealthy mindset, we will learn how to invent and create for the common good, through a spirit of collaboration. Then, we will learn that wealth not in tangible money, but in materialized ideas that have been brought about by study, discipline, determination and productivity.[18]

A wealth of contentment

The scriptures speak clearly concerning the gain which comes to an individual who is contented and has come to

---

[18] Ehimwenma E. Aimiuwu, the difference between wealth and riches, http://colorheritage.blogspot.com/

"rest" in God. Although this may sound difficult to believe and even stranger to hear, learning to be content with whatever situation you are in, by trusting in God's sovereignty and providence will make anyone far more wealthy than many of the materially rich people in the world. It was in this context that Paul gave his "straight talk" to Timothy:

" 6 But godliness actually is a means of great gain when accompanied by contentment. 7 For we have brought nothing into the world, so we cannot take anything out of it either. 8 If we have food and covering, with these we shall be content. 9 But those who want to get rich fall into temptation and a snare and many foolish and harmful desires which plunge men into ruin and destruction. 10 For the love of money is a root of all sorts of evil, and some by longing for it have wandered away from the faith and pierced themselves with many griefs. 11But flee from these things, you man of God, and pursue righteousness, godliness, faith, love, perseverance and gentleness."

(1Timothy 6:6-11 NASB)

Here we find a seven-fold admonition:

1. We are deceived if we assume that gain or material wealth is next to godliness.
2. Godliness with contentment is great gain.
3. We must always remember that we brought nothing into this world and that we can carry none of the stuff we have accumulated out.
4. Food and clothing are the essential things and we should be content with these.
5. We must avoid greed and lust which tempt, ensnare and destroy many who want to be rich.
6. We must at all costs avoid the love of money by loving God and people and making money a servant not a master.
7. We must be careful to avoid the deceitfulness of riches (Matthew 13:22) by following after righteousness, godliness, faith, love, patience and meekness.

One could interpret the above to mean that God has a problem with rich people, but this not so. God loves all people, rich and poor alike, but since the rich are in greater danger of being led astray, He warns them about the correct view and use of their material wealth.

" 17 Instruct those who are rich in this present world not to be conceited or to fix their hope on the *uncertainty of riches*, but on God, who richly supplies us with all things to enjoy. 18 Instruct them *to do good, to be rich in good works, to be generous and ready to share,* 19 storing up for themselves the treasure of a good foundation for the future, so that they may take hold of that which is life indeed." (1Timothy 6:17-19 NASB).

Could it be any clearer?

Our material wealth must be used for good.

Those whom God blesses with material wealth must be "rich in good works" and ready to give, especially to advance the cause of the poor, the underprivileged and the needy. Job in the Old Testament, blessed with much material wealth, is a good example to follow.

> " 13 The blessing of the one ready to perish came upon me,
> And I made the widow's heart sing for joy.
> 14 I put on righteousness, and it clothed me;
> My justice was like a robe and a turban.
> 15 *I was eyes to the blind*
> *And feet to the lame.*
> 16 *I was a father to the needy,*
> And I investigated the case which I did not know.
> 17 I broke the jaws of the wicked
> and snatched the prey from his teeth."
> (Job 29:13-17 NASB).

The apostle Paul spoke concerning this perfect balance in his own life.

> " 11 Not that I speak from want, for I have learned to be content in whatever circumstances I am. 12 I know how to get along with humble means, and I

also know how to live in prosperity; in any and every circumstance I have learned the secret of being filled and going hungry, both of having abundance and suffering need. 13 I can do all things through Him who strengthens me."
(Philippians 4:11-13 NASB).

This perfect balance is earmarked in the Book of Psalms.

"Better is the little of the righteous
Than the abundance of many wicked."
(Psalm 37:16 NASB)

" 33 Teach me, O LORD, the way of your statutes,
And I shall observe it to the end.
34 Give me understanding, that I may observe your law
And keep it with all my heart.
35 Make me walk in the path of your commandments,
For I delight in it.
36 Incline my heart to your testimonies

And not to dishonest gain.

37 Turn away my eyes from looking at vanity,

And revive me in your ways.

38 Establish your word to your servant,

As that which produces reverence for you.

39 Turn away my reproach which I dread,

For Your ordinances are good.

40 Behold, I long for your precepts;

Revive me through your righteousness."

(Psalm 119:33-40 NASB)

And again in the Book of Proverbs.

"There is one who pretends to be rich, but has nothing;

Another pretends to be poor, but has great wealth."

(Proverbs 13:7 NASB)

"Wealth obtained by fraud dwindles,

But the one who gathers by labor increases it."

(Proverbs 13:11 NASB)

"Great wealth is in the house of the righteous,
But trouble is in the income of the wicked."
(Proverbs 15:16 NASB)

"Better is a little with righteousness
than great income with injustice."

(Proverbs 16:8 NASB).

The words of Agur and his prayer to God drive home the point:

" 8 Keep deception and lies far from me,
Give me neither poverty nor riches;
Feed me with the food that is my portion,
9 That I not be full and deny you and say, "Who is the LORD?"
Or that I not be in want and steal,
And profane the name of my God."
(Proverbs 30:8-9 NASB)

Biblical prosperity simply means that you are successful at what you are endeavoring to do by the grace of God. It may involve a lot of money or it may not. Wealth can be obtained honestly or dishonestly, ethically or unethically. We must be careful not to harshly judge Christians and others whom God has blessed with material wealth since the success they have is because of the blessings they have received from Him. These are those who have worked hard, created value, applied biblical principles, expected God's blessings and received from him abundantly. I think it should also be said that we shouldn't judge Christians and others who do not have as much material blessings as others since contentment is still a key to a wealthy mindset.

Here are a few guidelines to follow in mastering the art of contentment:

- Choose to be content with what you have.
- Give thanks for everything.
- Meditate on the impermanence of wealth, reputation and worldly success.

- Be generous and give to others.

- Don't accumulate wealth while others starve.

- Avoid excesses.

- Value moderation.

- Rejoice.

- Pray continually.

- In everything give thanks. (1 Thess. 5:16,17 & Phil 4:4).

Epilogue

This book deals with the realm of money management and finance.

By His death on the cross and miraculous resurrection, Jesus defeated the principalities and is forever Lord of all things, all realms, visible and invisible, temporal and eternal. To God there is nothing secular, all things are spiritual.

The global recession is here. Some are saying that this is the "new normal"! We must remember the parable of the ant and the grasshopper. The ant is disciplined, gathering food in the summer when the harvest is plentiful and storing it in the lean winter months. The grasshopper "lives for today", eating and drinking everything in sight, partying as if the good times will never end. When winter arrives, the ant is prepared and survives. The grasshopper is doomed. The time of winter is here. Now is the time to learn about financial prudence, to learn how to be like the ant and to learn how to survive and thrive in this global recession by pursuing the God of wealth and true riches with a wealthy mind-set.

Money matters and we can learn to master it.

Bibliography

Aimiuwu Ehimwenma E, The difference between wealth and riches (http:/colorheritage.blogspot.com/)

Colander David C, Macroeconomics 4th edition (Mc Graw Hill, Irwin 2001, NY, NY)

Fraser Robert, Marketplace Christianity (New Grid Publishing, Kansas 2006)

Miller Darrow, Discipling Nations (YWAM Publishing 1998)

Otabil Mensa Dr, Four Laws of Productivity (The International Central Gospel Church, Ghana 1991)

Peacocke Dennis, Doing Business God's Way (Rebuild, Santa Rosa California 1995)

Proctor Bob, You were born Rich (Life Productions 1997)

Silbiger Steven, The Jewish Phenomenon (Longstreet Press, Atlanta Georgia 2000)

Silvoso Ed, Transformation (Regal Books 2007)

Sparks Austin T, The Purpose of God (www.austin-sparks.net/english/000417.html)

About the author

Ricardo Taylor is from the beautiful island of Barbados in the Caribbean. He is married to Denise Yolanda his wife of twenty four years. He and his wife are proud parents of three children. Ricardo attended the University of the West Indies (Cave Hill campus) in Barbados and graduated with a Bachelor of Science, honors degree in Accounting. He later qualified as a chartered accountant and has been working in business as a money manager ever since. Ricardo has pastored a local congregation in Barbados for over ten years but his passion and call is to the market place. It is important though to recognize that the market place is still a place, the church is a people, so he has an enduring passion for the simple church and the kingdom of God. He has authored one other book, Fully Equipped, by the Holy Spirit.

Other Books by Ricardo Taylor

Fully Equipped, by the Holy Spirit- Available at Amazon.com

You may reach Ricardo Taylor at the following ministry address:

New Ground International Barbados
PO Box 18070
Bottom Bay
St. Phillip
Barbados

Telephone 246-230-6361